SUDDENLY

PROPHETIC CROSSING OF THE END-TIME REVIVAL WATERS FOR THE LAST DAYS INGATHERING

REV. CHRIS MEIER

CCM4 Worldwide Worship Publishing

Suddenly
Copyright © 2021 by Rev. Chris Meier

To Contact the Author: www.suddenlybook.com or revchrismeier.com

Due to the nature of the Internet and its fluidity, URL references may not be the same as listed, having changed addresses. In that case, queries to a search engine of your choice may be required.

There are instances throughout this book where I mention our enemy's name, satan. I refuse to capitalize it. Call it artistic license, conviction or bad grammar, whichever you choose, but I still refuse to capitalize his name. The only time it might be, is when I quote directly from another publication, or at the beginning of a sentence.

All rights reserved. No part of this book may be used or reproduced in any manner without prior written permission.

All Scripture quotations, unless otherwise indicated, are taken from the King James Version (Authorized Version). Bible quotations designated (NET) are from the NET Bible, "Scripture quoted by permission. NET Bible, Registered, copyright 1996-2006 by Biblical Studies Press, L. L. C." http://netbible.com <https://bible.org><netbible.org> All rights reserved.

Book cover/jacket graphic design artist: Rachel Abou-Zeid
Cover artwork by: Jan Asleson, SpiritWingsDesigns.com

19.99 US dollars, Paperback

CCM4 Worldwide Worship Publishing
CCM4WorldwideWorship.Org

ISBN
978-1-7374605-1-0 (Hardcover)
978-1-7374605-4-1 (Paperback)
978-1-7374605-7-2 (eBook)

Table of Contents

1. We All Start Somewhere — 7
2. Church Life — 15
3. With Our Backs Against a Wall — 23
4. Overcoming Dangers Because of the Fear of the Lord — 31
5. The Traps — 39
6. Revival Regardless — 47
7. The Fear of the Lord — 57
8. The Grace of God — 63
9. The Seven-Fold Spirit of God — 71
10. True Judgment — 79
11. Possessing the Kingdom — 89
12. When the Bride is Compromised — 103
13. Revival to the Nations — 119
14. Hope in a Suddenly God: A God of Wholeness — 133
15. An Overflowing Outpouring: Revival to First Types — 147
16. Outpouring: Mankind — 159
17. Headwaters and The Bride — 173
18. First Things First and Then a Wedding Feast — 187
19. Ephesus — 197
20. The Galilean Wedding — 209
21. Final Thoughts — 215

Acknowledgements

To my dear friend in the Lord, Mickey, who, between a rock and a hard place, remained faithful in sharing the word of the Lord as we chewed on Isaiah 11 together, becoming a sweet 'smell' before Our Lord.

To Jan, turning the ethereal of seer prophets into visions of the saints that all mortals may behold.

To Rachel, thank you for praying; you have saved my bacon again.

To my forty-two year love, Bill: "Even the youths shall faint and be weary, and the young men shall utterly fall: But they that wait upon the LORD shall renew their strength; they shall mount up with wings as eagles; they shall run and not be weary; and they shall walk, and not faint" (Isaiah 40:30-31).

Hebrews 13:8: "Jesus Christ the same yesterday, and to day, and for ever."

Mark 16:19-20: "So then after the Lord had spoken unto them, he was received up into heaven, and sat on the right hand of God. And they went forth, and preached every where, the Lord working with them, and confirming the word with signs following, Amen."

*Acts 2:1-4: "And when the day of Pentecost was fully come, they were all with one accord in one place. And **suddenly** there came a sound from heaven as of a rushing mighty wind, and it filled all the house where they were sitting. And there appeared unto them cloven tongues like as of fire, and it sat upon each of them. And they were all filled with the Holy Ghost, and began to speak with other tongues, as the Spirit gave them utterance."*

Chapter One

We All Start Somewhere

I was saved in 1979, at the very end of the Jesus Movement, almost at the beginning of the Charismatic and "New" Charismatic Movements. My husband accepted Christ not long thereafter, sometime in early 1980. We were engaged at the time. Being a good Catholic, as well as a former choir boy, he had to make a decision whether or not to marry me since my salvation experience had been somewhat too intense for him. It did not fit into any of the religious understanding he had grown up with.

I was baptized in water in December of 1979, about two to three months after praying the sinner's prayer, during the autumn Jewish feasts. I came up out of the water with— as the church mothers called it— "utterance." Knowing what the word meant, I joked to myself that the church must have made some odd colloquialism for a new foot-and-mouth disease. I knew nothing about speaking with other tongues nor what its purpose was.

Since it was December in the northeastern part of the United States, the water as well as the church was a bit brisk. Many of those I had invited thought I was cold, thus making me shout out incomprehensibly due to the chill of the water. That was not the case. It was like I was in a warm bubble. I heard my pastor speaking, "In the Name of Jesus; in the Name of the Father and of the Son and of the Holy Spirit." The best way to describe it was like being in a womb. I was enveloped and totally vacuum-sealed with a warmth and power that carried me and cradled me.

It goes without saying that Jesus brought us to a good teaching pastor who taught classic Pentecostal theology, while we experienced signs and wonders as the Gospel was preached. We were taught plainly that signs and wonders attended the preaching of the Gospel (Mark 16:20). All this, as the local church flowed in the gifts of the Holy Spirit seen in Acts and taught by Paul in 1 Corinthians 12-14. The love of God was, and still is, at the center of all we do in Christ. We were bathed in His love as we were taught Jesus' deep love for people and the church, His bride.

Coming from a Catholic background and seeing the obvious change in my life, my fiancé had to decide whether or not this was theologically sound. He made the decision to attend Catholic mass on Sunday mornings and Bible studies with my Pentecostal pastor on Friday evenings. We were engaged for over a year and a quarter, so there was plenty of time for him to decide what he wanted to do. It took him three months, but at the end of those few months he gave me a simple announcement: He would be attending that little Pentecostal Church, and my pastor would become his pastor and we would be married there. That would become our church. He would be leaving the Catholic Church. And that was, as they say, that!

His decision didn't come without some supernatural experiences of his own. Before he saw me with his own eyes, Jesus gave him a dream in which he saw my face. He was told I was to be his wife. So when we met months later, he was a bit more patient with me than he would have been with any other woman. I say that because I had been a bit of a wild child as well as an enterprising teenager. Some of my endeavors took me into areas that were a bit too over the top for him.

Bill has never been drunk a day in his life; never smoked or did anything else that wasn't healthy. He was into weight-lifting and loved all things cars and trucks; frankly, anything that moved on wheels.

Without that dream, I don't think he would have stayed around for those few months we dated before my salvation experience.

I certainly don't think he would have left Catholicism either. There was a holiness in his family. He lived in his parents' house but had the whole upstairs apartment to himself. When I visited, there was a fragrance from the Holy Spirit that manifested physically as fruity flowers, though I can't say exactly what the perfume was. It was like flowers that were not from this Earth. We talked about it at that time. He said he felt it was the angel that was there since no one cleaned the place with any detergent and no one wore any perfume that would explain the fragrance. It came and went as well. Since the windows were closed, and we never smelled it anywhere but inside the apartment, we knew it couldn't have come from the outside. It more or less surrounded him each time he knew God spoke.

It goes without saying that I was not his mother's favorite person during that time. She blamed me for taking him away from his church and felt I was a "bad" influence. Without Christ's salvation, she would not have been wrong. His family attended the wedding but refused to speak to me and refused to go to the reception afterwards.

I will say this though, I respected her to the utmost for what she did years later. It may have been one or possibly two years after we married, but she was the kind of woman who admitted mistakes. She came up to me after a Sunday family dinner at their house and asked for my forgiveness for how they treated me. I'll never forget her words of kindness: "I was wrong; you have been very good for Bill and I'm grateful for how happy he is and how much he has changed." It takes a big woman to admit something like that. I loved her dearly. She had a sweet spirit and a big heart, which her son reflects to me each and every day of our forty-plus years of marriage.

My religious upbringing was not as monogamous as my husband's. My mother's father had studied to be a Catholic priest, but left the priesthood's schooling when he decided to marry. He attended mass somewhat regularly. His wife, my grandmother, had been raised Anglican but couldn't find such a church in the neighborhood; so, she attended an Episcopalian church: But only when necessary! When my mother married my father she promised to raise us Lutheran, as was his family's religion. Quite frequently, we lived in Jewish neighborhoods. This meant we went to a Catholic Church occasionally while we attended the closest Lutheran Church's Sunday school.

I read from the Bible as a child in my spare time, though I got lost when it came to all the 'who-begets-who' in the Old Testament. When my mother remarried, she married a Baptist who agreed to go to Lutheran Church. My friends were almost all Jewish. I went to Friday night sabbath meals. Since I was reading and learning from the Bible regularly, gleaned a tiny bit about Anglicans, Episcopalians and Baptists while attending Lutheran congregations and lived and breathed among Jews, it was only natural for me to ask my mother if I could attend synagogue. To say she freaked would not quite explain her reaction.

I overheard her conversation with my grandmother, the sometime Anglican-Episcopalian. "Mother, what should I do with her? I fear she's going to become a nun." My Nana had some wise words for her daughter. "Harriet, don't worry. At least it's all the same God from the same book. It could be worse, she could get involved in something wacky. Let her go to synagogue with her Jewish friends; it can't hurt." My mother's reaction was quite clear: "Absolutely not." That began a time period where she campaigned for my extra-curricular activities. In her mind, I wasn't busy enough; Girl Scouts, sports, school work, and particularly horses. I loved horses, and still live with them.

A smart woman, all that activity did the trick. I became so busy with school work and horses that I really didn't give synagogue attending any further thought. Unfortunately, all that activity didn't prepare me for the tragedy our family would soon go through. My mother's second marriage collapsed. Not long thereafter, my grandfather died. This sent her into a period of depressive pain from which she never recovered. He had been the bulwark patriarch of the family. Strong and kind, he had a sturdy work ethic. These several and sudden tragedies took out three breadwinners within a short period of time, leaving my grandmother as our sole support. A trained professional, her paycheck wasn't small, but it also wasn't enough to take on the new tasks required to keep us from poverty.

I'm not sure how we made it. Looking back, I know Jesus sustained us. Being the oldest child, I felt the need to step up and earn something. As soon as I could, I got the odd jobs available to someone in their early teens. As I got into my later teens, the needs became more acute, hence, part-time side jobs. Realizing I could not sustain my life nor whatever needs might be required of me for the family's future, I knew I needed a good paying career. I had a three-step plan: court-reporting school, get a job and save up enough money to go to veterinarian college; graduate veterinarian college and— voilà— solid career! At no time during those steps was there a plan for Jesus.

I was still some years from my career goals and needed to find a better paying job. Back in those days getting a disarticulated ID for work was all the rage, and it was fairly easy. The government had so many loopholes within different departments, that by following one of them, the state would actually help you. With it in hand, I got two jobs; one after school from four to eleven answering phones at a local take-out, and one tending bar for twelve hours on Sundays.

It was during step one of my plan that I came to take a new friend home from school. Her ride died and I was always looking for someone to share the fuel costs. What I didn't know was that she was a backslidden Christian. What she didn't know was that Jesus was going to call her out of her apostasy. Her mom had six children from several different men. They lived in the projects, in government-subsidized apartments. I only had to travel five or so miles to drop her off at home each day.

We were both excited about becoming court stenographers and talked endlessly about all the things young woman talk about:

Suddenly

clothes, family, school, jobs, guys and parties. And, there were parties. She was a party girl. I was in-between boy friends, deciding they took up too much of my time. To be where I needed my life to go, boys had to be kept to a minimum. Friends were okay, but anything more serious had to be shown the door.

This was where my life had taken me when I met my husband. I didn't return his first call, and he wasn't going to call me again. If it wasn't for that dream he had with the face he saw (mine), he wouldn't have. At the same time, one of my other girlfriends told me to give him a second look. She said plainly, "He is so hot; if you don't go out with him, I will!" She was, of course, right. I did take a second look. We hit it off and kept dating while I continued with school and he worked. His work ethic and clean living were good for both of us.

One Friday while driving my party-girl, car-pooling friend home from school, she told me her story of being a back-slidden Christian and how Jesus was now back in her life. She shared quite a bit with me on that ride home that challenged my ideas and plans. Since Bill and I were heading up north to the lake for the weekend, I planned to pray to Jesus while I was alone in the woods. I did that all weekend long and nothing happened. I thought at least something should happen. I knew as a child I had seen many spiritual events in and around church. That's because each and every time I prayed as a youngster "stuff" happened. In fact, it scared me so much that I decided to keep it a little less intense, withdrawing from that kind of prayer. It was natural for me to assume as an adult something would happen, especially after listening to my friend's experience of coming back to Jesus.

Monday afternoon on our drive home from school, I told her nothing happened after praying. She asked me if I confessed with my mouth to anyone else, since that was part and parcel of being "led to the Lord" (Romans 10:9-10). I said I had not. So we did that immediately. She led me in the sinner's prayer. Maybe it wasn't such a wise thing to be driving a car. I had to pull over. What I now know to be the tangible, fiery presence of the Holy Spirit invaded the vehicle.

We All Start Somewhere

We were both overcome. We were both laughing and crying and shaking, all at the same time! I'm still not sure exactly how I drove home.

It had been such a "suddenly" experience that reminded me of all my previous childhood experiences with God. He was just too much. He overcame all my walls and did it so quickly that I felt overcome and thoroughly loved and accepted. My husband's experience was different, but no less overcoming and "suddenly." He accepted Jesus about six months after I did. It took about five years for him to have an overcoming moment with God. He had never been filled with the Holy Spirit with the evidence of speaking in other tongues until one Sunday morning service.

By then we were in a different Pentecostal Church. Out of the corner of my eye as I was worshipping, I saw what looked like electricity hit him, flowing through his body. As he shook, he sort of hit the pew with the seat of his pants. Since things like that happened all the time in that little church, I thought nothing of it. Later that day at home, I realized he had his prayer language.

Almost immediately I started having dreams of me living during the end times. Our pastor taught us what Christians call eschatology, or the church during the last days. We were taught Jesus' return was imminent. Father God started showing me things in the word that I didn't know were connected. It took almost ten years before I even understood what He was showing me. There is nothing new under the sun. He speaks the same thing in each generation. Each new group of believers experiences a revival. Jesus shows them things about His return as they wait for Him.

This book is my best attempt to share what Jesus has shown me over the last forty years concerning an elongated period of time in what the body of Christ has called a last revival harvest before Jesus' return.

Suddenly

Proverbs 19:11: "A person's wisdom makes him slow to anger, and it is his glory to overlook an offense" (NET Bible).

Chapter Two

Church Life

We all experience Christ as we invite Him in; repenting and confessing our sins and asking the Holy Spirit to lead and guide us into all truth. To say we all experience that the same exact way would be untrue. As you can see from the previous chapter, my religious experiences and my husband's were quite different. Nevertheless, we both experienced Christ's salvation and the infilling of the Holy Spirit. We both followed the pattern seen in the New Testament.

Like the characters written about in the New Testament, our lives' stories are different. Yet, at some point in those lives, Christ suddenly impacts them, changing them forever. Is the walk always easy? Obviously, not; but it is revealing. We all begin a revelation in learning the truths exposed from the Old Testament's shadow of Messiah, to the New Testament's proclamation, appearance and transformation of Christ in our own lives. For this to happen, we have to learn. That means we must read our Bibles. We must be taught by the elders. It means we are going to experience church. This, of course, is where controversy will take place. As different as we are as people, there are different churches.

All New Testament Christian churches must follow a similar pattern as all Christian people must. The New Testament's Gospel of Jesus Christ must be preached. Solid doctrine must be taught and followed. The foremost thing a church must do to remain a pure and unspotted bride of Christ is to live, function and remain in the power of the Holy Spirit.

This book is not meant to teach the rudimentary doctrines of Christianity (see Hebrews 6:1-3). It is simply a sensing I have from the Holy Spirit what many years of end-time revivals will start to look like. I believe we will see thirty to forty years of revivals. It is possible in many circles that they have already started; and, it is possible that we haven't seen anything yet! One constant is that they will all experience and flow in the Holy Spirit in various signs and wonders. Whatever those Bible-based manifestations of the Holy Spirit, the key outreach must be souls. That's because the harvest will be massive. The harvest must be massive. We must all carry out our missions to share Christ with many souls.

If we are going to do that, we must go to church. As there are no perfect people, there are no perfect churches. One of my pastors used to say, "If you're looking for the perfect church, as soon as you find it and step through the doors, it becomes an imperfect church." Even though that's true, we as church elders cannot use that reality to be anything less than the true bride of Christ. That means the Holy Spirit will correct us. In order to do that, we must be open to Him. We must be reading our Bibles and we must be praying together to hear what it is that the Spirit is saying to the church.

My husband and I pastored a house church for eleven years. Even before that time, we offended the traditional mainline church. If you think me teaching, preaching and taking care of the upfront work would make them feel better, you are sorely mistaken. Bill did everything else: he cleaned, took care of the house, took care of the yard, did all necessary repairs as well as counseled the men. He led prayer meeting when necessary, being the head intercessor. In other words, he did most of the behind-the-scenes work. Of course, we overlapped each other's assignments as well. Trust me when I tell you that it seemed like we offended every pastor, church and Neanderthal available because of how we functioned. People who went to

Church Life

our church were told we were some kind of cult. Believe it or not, this was the easy persecution.

Once I accepted Christ, any and all sinful behaviors were gone. Being a choir boy, my husband may have had less to repent for, but he did repent. There was no known sin in our lives or doctrinal error; so the enemy of our souls tried to get the religious crowd to hate us for every lie he could pull off. The Lord showed me— almost immediately after salvation— not to get offended by anyone. The lessons He taught me then served me well years later, long before anyone wrote any books on the subject!

When all doors would be closed for me to serve the local congregation, the Lord would always open doors for ministry on the streets. Street ministry was always my favorite venue. Deliverance and inner healing became a ministry the Lord granted my husband and myself early on. We learned very quickly not to allow any bitterness or other roots to defile us or those around us (Hebrews 12:14-15). We learned how important God's grace is and the protection it, as well as the blood of Jesus holds for the saints (Deuteronomy 29:18-19).

I do recall one time just before we opened the church where my husband was working over the engine compartment of a car. I stopped off at the shop for some reason. He looked up and asked me how I was doing. I told him I could be better. He looked down at what seemed to be a mangled mess of metal and said, "You know, if this was 150 years ago, they would have burned you at the stake by now." I chuckled at that thought and said, "Thank God they're not allowed to do that anymore! But you do know if they burned me, you'd be right behind me. The only thing that might save you is the fact that you're a man!"

The truth is, if we want to get offended, we always can. The reality is, we've got to shrug it off and be about our Father's business. We can't sit idle, off in a corner licking our wounds. Jesus died to set humanity free. That means the devil is not going to give any of us a run up the ice to score any goals. He is going to try to fight us for each and every soul we see transformed. I am not implying that we should ignore being hurt by anyone. It is critically important that we share these wounds with those we are close with who have shown themselves trusted and honorable ministers. Confession, prayer, the blood of Jesus and His name are practices we must employ when we find areas of defilement or wounding affecting us.

As I've been sitting before the Lord, I keep sensing this great end-time revival. As I've said, He has shown me it will last many years. It will be the book of Acts all over again. What was the book of Acts all about? Primarily, it was the disciples of Jesus teaching and training or discipling the early church in the things of Christ— the word of God — and in the Holy Spirit. These, in turn, were sent out to transform many regions of the world. Signs and wonders accompanied the preaching of the Gospel. We must also disciple God's people from the word and the Holy Spirit. We must make sure they function in the gifts the Holy Spirit has given them and then we must send them out to where the lost souls are that they will meet.

We can't go out with a chip on our shoulders because so and so did us wrong. Certainly, that doesn't mean I need to keep myself in an abusive or defiling situation. But it does mean I need to forgive. I need to extend the forgiveness Jesus extended to me. It may mean I no longer associate with certain people. There is nothing wrong with leaving such situations as part and parcel of my choice to forgive them. If we look at each offending situation without anger, it is possible that many of them can teach us something about people, ourselves and our God. We can either see these times as opportunities or we can remain bitter. The choice really is ours to make. Forgiveness is a choice I make, not a feeling I have. Waiting to feel like forgiving someone will probably mean that we will never forgive anyone.

I certainly don't want to leave the impression that every Christian or church is a magnet for offense. We were members of some pretty special churches where the glory of God flowed like a river. We had some pretty awesome experiences in those churches. Some were larger and others were quite small where only heaven recorded their names. But we all must make a decision to walk in forgiveness to see that healing power of the cross extended to all we come in contact with.

If I've been healed by Jesus, that means I can keep being healed by the power of the Holy Spirit in whatever manner I need healing. Healing is the children's bread. In at least two of those churches we were miraculously healed. My husband and I have never had to go to doctors for healing. We have always been miraculously healed by the Spirit. So in 2019, when Jesus told me to go for elective surgery, I was not expecting it. In fact, that was totally unexpected and so totally wrong for my theology. Nine months later when my husband needed to go for surgery, it was not the normal experience for either one of us.

We have never wavered from belief in the word that, 'by His stripes I was healed' (1 Peter 2:24). I am not of the theological opinion that God sends any sickness to teach us anything. You would never break a child's leg or a pet's body in order to teach them something. First, that behavior is counterproductive to learning. Second, it is evil and sadistic; and third, it is unscriptural. What I am trying to convey is the lesson I was able to learn from some very difficult situations in which I had to rely on human healing for a short period of time.

I can't have any attitudes concerning those who must seek healing from our present health systems. In a little over a year, I went from someone who never saw a doctor for much of anything to experiencing six surgeries, three of which were major. Bill would experience one major surgery. It wasn't because we were so healthy that we never went to doctors. It was because Jesus healed us of every issue we had. Being forced to come to the reality of human healing, I am even more adamant than ever for divine healing.

Nevertheless, we accept God's people where they are and wash them in the word as the Holy Spirit directs. God's word is always a NOW word. It's not in the sweet by and by. It is now; it is for today and it will accomplish all it is sent out to do (Isaiah 55:11). We must receive it by faith. As we share the Gospel, we will always see healings and signs and wonders take place. We expect miracles. For us, there is nothing else to expect.

The first aspect of this end-time revival will be souls; the next will be signs and wonders to accompany that word. We truly change environments wherever the Gospel is preached. We must always be ready to forgive. We must easily forsake casting judgment concerning where people should be in their faith walk with Christ; lest, by our attitudes we become unable to enter this promised land of revival.

Suddenly

1 Corinthians 1:9-10: "*Indeed we felt as if the sentence of death had been passed against us, so that we would not trust in ourselves, but in God who raises the dead. He delivered us from so great a risk of death, and he will deliver us. We have set our hope on him that he will deliver us yet again*" (*NET Bible*).

Chapter Three

With Our Backs Against A Wall

God has always used times of trouble to come to His people. We read from the Bible that the end times will become a tremendous time of trouble (2 Timothy 3:1). So much so that people will run to God and the people of God (Zechariah 8:20-23). But there are other times of trouble this earth and her people of various countries have gone through. Since God's people live among many people groups, God's people have gone through quite a bit of tumult. We're told before the worst of the trouble, our Lord will rapture out His bride from this earth (1 Corinthians 15; 1 Thessalonians 4:13-5:11).

Rarely do we realize while reading the Gospels what it was like for the Jews, considering the kind of trouble a free Jewish people felt with Rome breathing down their backs. It was to this environment Messiah came the first time. Rarely do we understand what it was like for the Jewish nation to be enslaved by Egypt. Or, what it was like to be controlled in what you ate, how you worked and even where you lived. It was in that environment Moses came on the scene. And so it has been throughout biblical history: Joseph, Daniel, Esther, along with countless other names and historical stories.

In America we have such a history. We are a people who initially settled among Native Americans. We came from all over Europe, Africa — and more recently other places— to live without kings and nobility telling us what to do: A government to be formed by the people and for the people. In order for any people group to maintain that kind of government, they must know of such a history. They must also know what skills it took to gain such freedoms. In order to overcome and swallow up such a free people, it would stand to reason that any occupying force must remove that particular history and remove the skills needed to maintain it from functional memory.

As we live right now, the attempt to remove historical truth is taking place. This book is not meant to prove a communist takeover of America, or the world, for that matter. With any skill through Internet sleuthing, you should be able to find the evidence. Of course, you will have to remove Google as your search engine to get started. You will also have to be aware of the algorithms used in your apps and the malware uploaded on your hardware to try to prevent you from accessing such information. A lesson in computer technology couldn't hurt. If you're not into taking the time needed for such research, there are good books out there you can read. I've written one with a distinct warning from the Lord.[1]

When God speaks, the face of the earth hears Him. Because of some refusal on the part of a majority of the church to hear God on certain issues, the world hears and tries to do it. Unfortunately, not being filled with the Spirit of God, they cannot maintain God's directive. Instead, or quite often, the devil infiltrates, throwing his narrative into the mix. He needs humans attacking humans or church people attacking church people to get what he wants.

I say this because you know a pandemic is not about science when there are literally five different medical treatments available to actually stop a virus, but you never hear about them while millions of

---

[1] Meier, Chris, "70 Years of American Captivity: The Polity of God, The Birth of a Nation and The Betrayal of Government." 2016. Tellwell Publishers, Vancouver, British Columbia, Canada. In ebook, paperback and hardcover. Amazon link: < https://www.amazon.com/70-Years-American-Captivity-Government/dp/1773021141 >

people die needlessly.² You know it's not about the science when civil rights can be removed to force mask wearing, especially when certain virus particles are smaller than many masks out there.³ You know it's not about the science when you can go to the liquor store, the grocery or Home Depot, but attending a church service inside a parked car in the church's parking lot gets you arrested and the church shut down.⁴

You know it's not about social justice when rioters can burn down the businesses and homes of the marginalized populations the social justice says they are fighting for without any reprisals, or arrests. In fact, these same politicians promoting the curtailment of your rights to peaceful living, tell you that they'll pay for any reprisals those rioters might face, even though those riots burn down half a nation.⁵

Yet, when idiots get together and riot inside the workplace of the politicians, all of a sudden the FBI and the National Guard get involved, arresting hundreds. Don't misunderstand me; NO riot should go unpunished. I just feel the reason why someone riots to destroy life and property is irrelevant to the equal execution of arrests. Both groups of rioters should be arrested, regardless of why they riot.

---

2 < americasfrontlinedoctors.org >< https://medicalkidnap.com/2020/12/09/i-cant-keep-watching-patients-die-needlessly-medical-professor-testifies-to-congress-that-covid-cure-already-exists-with-ivermectin/ >< https://covid19-criticalcare.com > < https://americasfrontlinedoctors.org/frontlinenews/urgent-british-report-calls-for-complete-cessation-of-covid-vaccines-in-humans/ > accessed 6/19/21.

3 < aflds.org >< aapsonline.org >

4 https://www1.cbn.com/cbnnews/2020/april/dont-trample-the-constitution-churchgoers-fined-500-by-police-for-sitting-in-their-cars-with-windows-closed accessed 6/19/21

5 < https://www.foxnews.com/politics/aoc-ocasio-cortez-ayanna-pressley-bail-counter-protesters-boston-straight-pride-parade-squad >< https://www.oregonlive.com/news/2020/06/whos-behind-the-portland-protest-bail-fund-thats-raised-more-than-500000.html > sites accessed 6/19/21.

Suddenly

That's how you know a stronghold is evident. That's how you know a lie is being told in order to effectuate a certain outcome. The church has maintained a Jezebel spirit in both denying the Spirit of God in power, signs and wonders and in sleeping with the devil in sexual sin. A Jezebel spirit is easy to kick off of someone flowing in Godly power. Once we are compromised, it becomes harder, but not impossible. What makes this thing so insidious is when it marries or becomes joined to a Babylonian spirit.

In my first book, 'Beyond Strongholds, Infiltration by the Glory of God,' I go in-depth into Old Testament Jezebel. What made her powerful was her marriage to legitimacy by marrying an Israeli King. She was a daughter of Tyre. When these sexual spirits try to gain power they always go to governing/religious spiritual forces to get it. Here in America, this isn't necessary. Why? Because we are very much like the book of Judges; we do what is right in our own eyes. In this case, we have a national narrative of allowing people to do their own thing as long as they don't harm someone else.

As Thomas Jefferson once said, "But our rulers can have no authority over such natural rights, only as we have submitted to them. The rights of conscience we never submitted, we could not submit. We are answerable for them to God. The legitimate powers of government extend to such acts only as are injurious to others. But it does me no injury for my neighbor to say there are twenty gods, or no god. It neither picks my pocket nor breaks my leg."[6]

So it matters very little for people to join to whom they please. They must stand before God and give an account for what they have done in this life like all the rest of us. If someone's religion forbids such

---

[6] Thomas Jefferson, "Query XVII, Notes on the State of Virginia" In "The Works of Thomas Jefferson" Edited by H.A. Washington. Volume 8; 400. (New York: Townsend Mac Coun. 1884)

action, then leave the faithful alone. The human genome has already been mapped. There is no science supporting a new gender.[7]

There is no harm to anyone for churches to say no to blessing what they believe are immoral actions. At the same time, no one should dictate who people decide to join with. Since we all stand before God for our own actions, there should be no war here on earth surrounding these issues. Children should not be involved in such action. Research doesn't absolve anyone when children are involved any more than divorce in traditional unions does. Once someone is of legal age, they should be able to decide their own life choices.

Nevertheless, the devil and social-communists need this war to go on. They must get rid of the church in some way. These issues will do nicely. Now, the devil doesn't know exactly what God is going to do to deliver a people. He just knows if the people are around that can bring deliverance, he must do something to get rid of them. The pattern of Israel and her neighbors are our best biblical example for that.

In order to take out a nation of God's people, the devil has always used this Jezebel, quasi-religious Babylonian spirit to do so. The book of Esther gives us an Old Testament example. We will look at her example shortly. For now, what I'd like to concentrate on, are the patterns God employs to give His people the encouragement necessary to step into marvelous revival waters if, or when, such traps arise.

Why does He wait until our backs are up against the proverbial wall or Red Sea? Speculation here won't help anyone. But I can say what the Bible says. When the Israelites had their backs against pharaoh's army and their faces toward the impossibility of crossing the Red Sea, Moses told them to, "Fear ye not, stand still, and see the salva-

---

[7] < https://www.geneticliteracyproject.org/2015/10/12/despite-what-you-may-have-read-theres-no-gay-gene/ > The previous is a quick and unbiased article. The second one is more involved with various overtones, but the science is still good. < https://www.trueorigin.org/gaygene01.php > accessed 6/19/21.

tion of the Lord, which he will shew to you to day: for the Egyptians whom ye have seen to day, ye shall see them again no more for ever. The Lord shall fight for you, ye shall hold your peace" (Exodus 14:13-14).

There is something about in-your-face faith. You experience it. No one can move you off of it. Facing impossible situations that only God can save you in, through or from causes the kind of faith no one can talk you out of. Americans experienced this kind of faith when faced with the impossibility of a world power in England desiring to overcome and control us. For over 150 years after, the stories of the Revolutionary War carried many patriots. They were brothers and sisters in their knowledge of a God who rescued and saved. But like any faith, it must be experienced by the people who exercise it. Our mothers and fathers cannot experience faith for us.

We have neglected those skills necessary in maintaining the political as well as the religious covenant our early American mothers and fathers left us in our three governing documents: The Declaration of Independence, The Constitution and The Bill of Rights. In many situations, we have ignored the religious covenant they saw from the Bible. It was that same covenant early Israel followed to become a nation of freedom loving people. It is this pattern of political covenant that keeps the American nation humming. It is the pattern of religious covenant which keeps God's people free to worship Him, while trusting His ability to rescue us when we cannot rescue ourselves.

It becomes necessary to profess this with our mouths and teach the next generation these traditions, along with the factual evidence of their benefits. This is what our enemies cannot ignore. They can try to control the retelling on social media or elsewhere by calling it racist, but they cannot ignore the factual outcome of covenant's effects. We must not be negative about our faith or our God's ability to rescue us. We must take positive action to present ourselves as living sacrifices so God may alight on our lives, bringing His redeeming presence with Him to the banquet table (Romans 12:1-3).

With Our Backs Against A Wall

This brings me to the other pattern of a kinsman redeemer. We will review this more in depth in our next chapter. But for now, God wanted to make sure that none of His people's families were left without a remnant name within Israel's tribes. To that end, if a family line was about to die out, one of its closest relatives had the right or ability to "buy back" or redeem the land and wealth of their tribal relatives. To that end, the genetic line would also be maintained by raising up seed to their relative. In this way, family heritage continued.

For the church today, as well as Christians from yesteryear, the typology is clear. Jesus became our Kinsman Redeemer, buying us back from lifestyles of sin and degradation and giving us an inheritance from His Father. This redemption purchased us, giving us a new Father and family. We now become members of God's family with all the benefits of firstborn children, never to be removed from the beloved body of Christ.

Christ's blood is what enables a New Covenant to surround us. Our acceptance of Jesus' blood as payment for our sin enables all the wealth, ancestral as well as legal and biblical benefits to flow from Jesus' Father— as our New Father, the Ancient of Days— to us, His new children.

It is exactly at that moment when it looks as if our backs against the wall will kill us, that God comes to save and redeem. He does what no one else will or can do: He totally saves and rescues. As Moses said, all we need to do is stand and watch the salvation of our God. Now, that will cause a revival. Wow; what a Father and what an Elder Brother and friend we have in Jesus!

Suddenly

*2 Corinthians 5:11: "Therefore, **because we know the fear of the Lord,** we try to persuade people, but we are well known to God, and I hope we are well known to your consciences too."*

Chapter Four

Overcoming Dangers Because Of The Fear Of The Lord

As a people, we must hear from God and we must know when we do, that He is speaking and He is faithful to perform what He says He will do. We must also know the saints who speak, as well. In times past within our churches, especially those of us who were raised up in prophetic, evangelism-based Pentecostal churches, we knew who spoke the word of the Lord and we were known of each other.

Today's church Online is not the same. I never make it a habit to view many ministries and churches on YouTube. Why, you might ask? Because I don't know them. I only view those ministers and ministries which I have a knowledge of the leadership or people within the congregation. I view ministers the Holy Spirit has confirmed to me by the word and the Spirit. Many times I will view such things when they are sent to me by trusted Christian intercessors. Even then, I view it all with a very clear and sharp eye. I don't swallow everything sent to me.

In fact, recently I was quite stunned with what I saw. Since intercessors will send me new words, et cetera, on my phone, I view it from that platform. So I don't normally get what's next in the queue from sites like YouTube. One day I happened to be on my computer. Because I logged in that way, YouTube gave me more site information and I could see other similar, expressive videos in a very long queue.

I was absolutely flabbergasted. Everyone had a word or a vision. Everyone wanted the "next big-word" status and its popularity. This is the problem when we allow unbelievers to host the church. This was not, nor is it the church as I know it, nor is it the proper way to conduct prophetic ministry according to the Bible. As a result, the potential for falsity is great.

In 1 Corinthians, Paul gives parameters for prophetic words. Not only that, he says when one speaks, others should listen and judge. We're told tongues and interpretation of tongues is for unbelievers. I've learned as I've pastored many prophetic meetings that as a matter of course, gifts of prophecy should be limited to no more than three. Dreams, visions, receiving a psalm or song, should, in my opinion, function the same way. One at a time and limited. The Spirit of God will never interrupt the Spirit of God. You would never blurt out a gift of prophecy or other word in the middle of someone speaking, or a sermon. We always honored the Holy Spirit by giving Him a time during the worship for such words. But once that time is up and the Lord has shifted the meeting, "the spirits of the prophets are subject to the prophets" (1 Corinthians 14:29-33).

We have to function in humility, order, courtesy and discretion. When we don't function within biblical values, we risk spending the whole meeting with various words that circle us. Instead of celebrate Christ when we come together, we wind up chasing our tails, so to speak. Instead of telling us where we are going for the week ahead and preparing the body of Christ for things or battles to come, we leave unprepared and unfulfilled because we have moved in chaos instead of Holy Spirit-filled, Godly order.

When we understand **the fear of the Lord,** we know those who move in the same context. Because of this, we persuade those who don't know Jesus. Because of this, our attention is directed to pleasing God, not man, but we are known to one another as those who please our Lord. Because many churches wish to silence fifty percent of the Lord's army, signs and wonders are nonexistent in many of them.

As a result, an excuse must be made as to why they don't see God moving supernaturally.[8] It is this excuse from a human perspective that looks like it turned into a doctrine of demons. Frankly, I think the demon was there all along, it was just exposed once the doctrine went into practical usage among the churches who followed its teaching. That doctrine says that God stopped moving in signs and wonders as soon as the early disciples died. This makes absolutely no sense. Before the disciples were ever born, God was moving in signs and wonders (Genesis 1; Exodus 14; 1 Kings 17-21; this is just a handful). Why would He stop now? He wouldn't; Jesus Christ is the same, yesterday, today and forever (Hebrews 13:8).

One could say that signs and wonders do not make a church, and I would agree. Seeing souls saved and set free does, though; and, that is the best sign and wonder for me. These doctrines of demons have a very seductive and eventually debilitating effect. Over time, many of these churches no longer see souls saved. They eventually no longer disciple according to biblical standards; and, that produces an effect among the congregants of no longer reading their Bibles. This is how you know that somewhere along the line a belief system was introduced that is a doctrine from the pit of hell.

So a few of our pitfalls have become evident: Hindering the body of Christ due to gender or race and the second, hindering all of God's

---

[8] This is only one aspect of not discerning the Lord's body that we see from Paul's message in 1 Corinthians 11:29. The first is not acknowledging the bread as a symbol of His body, whipped and beaten for our healing (Isaiah 53:5; 1 Peter 2:24). The second is not understanding the various gifts we see within our distinct members from our various churches (Romans 12; 1 Corinthians 12-14; Ephesians 4). I believe the last is a place of discrimination where we look at gender or ethnic cultures or even economic stature, and we use those differences to hinder the gift that God gives us in the form of people to further the work of the Lord (James 1:27-3:2; 1 Timothy 6:1-19).

Suddenly

people due to doctrines of demons (2 Timothy 3:5). The third is moving in God's gifts improperly; this allows falsity to become evident among us. In 2020, Jesus told me plainly that those people caught up in these false doctrines were going to get saved. That tells me how needed this revival is.

In the previous chapter I mentioned God's pattern of rescuing us with revival in glory as we are about to be swallowed up by our enemy, the devil. I mentioned our lack of acknowledging our covenant relationships as a pitfall we suffer from. This error allows our enemy, satan,[9] access to us in ways too numerous to mention. Let's look at one of those dangerous pitfalls overtaking the modern church which hinders revival.

The story of Ruth is a story where the death of a family line would have meant the death of a nation because Ruth became the mother of Obed, and Obed became the father of Jesse, and Jesse became the father of King David. If a kinsman redeemer had not been willing to rescue Ruth and Naomi, all would have been lost. In fact, David would not have been born. We know Ruth to have lived during the time period of the Judges. She was a Moabite who married an Israelite who died after leaving Israel. She would not leave her mother-in-law, Naomi, desiring to return with her to the land of Israel.

By refusing to leave Naomi, she, by all appearances would be giving up the ability to have a husband or family. She makes this declaration to Naomi as the reason why: "And Ruth said, Intreat me not to leave thee, or to return from following after thee: for whither thou goest, I will go; and where thou lodgest, I will lodge: thy people shall be my people, and thy God my God: Where thou diest, will I die, and there will I be buried: the LORD do so to me, and more also, if ought but death part thee and me" (Ruth 1:16-17).

---

[9] No, the fact that satan's name is not capitalized is not a typo on my part. I refuse to capitalize anything about him, including his name.

Overcoming Dangers Because Of The Fear Of The Lord

We know many things within the first chapter surrounding the story of these holy women, but three of those things are integral for the generations after them, and for us today. One, they lived during the time of the Judges in Israel (v. 1). The book of Judges tells us that during that time period, "In those days there was no king in Israel: every man did that which was right in his own eyes" (Judges 21:25). This last verse of the book of Judges reads right into Verse 1 in the book of Ruth. While we could assume they did what they thought was right because no king told them what to do, it seems to be more intense than that. The understanding here is that they did what they thought, not what God thought was right. It was a man-based thought society, not one centered on the word of the Lord.

The next thing we know about these women is that they were holy. They did not seek husbands from a land of strangers. Instead of taking the easy road, they returned to the land of Israel because "she had heard in the country of Moab how that the LORD had visited his people in giving them bread" (Ruth 1:6). And lastly, we know that they feared the Lord. Ruth states plainly to Naomi, "Thy people shall be my people and thy God my God."

I'm not trying to run down the modern church, but we must stop becoming like the world and start fearing the Lord. We do what we feel is right in our own eyes, instead of what our Lord has written. We take the easy road in many areas, not willing to do things God's way. Everyone always likes a winner. But the reality is Jesus finds us and those we are called to minister to in anything but winning ways. Quite often, we come to the Lord in the depths of our despair. In order to receive all God has for us, we will have to identify with Him. We will need to fear the Lord as the Bible lays out for us.

We're going to look at some key elements in a healthy fear of the Lord. For now, we know its benefit leads us into wisdom, and not just any wisdom, but Godly wisdom (Psalm 111:10; Proverbs 9:10). Let me ask a redundant question. How many pitfalls, dangers and traps can we avoid with an attitude displaying a healthy fear of the Lord? This is a key element in seeing revival flow for generations, not just a few months or years here and there.

It is also a treasure trove of spiritual wealth after we make a commitment to accept Christ's sacrifice. It helps us hear clearly from the Holy Spirit; unclogging years of mind games we get ourselves involved with so easily. When we move in Godly fear, with the Holy Spirit wooing us into all truth (John 16:13-15), we aren't negatively impacted by spiritual events. We easily learn the New Testament's parameters for such things, eagerly desiring spiritual gifts (1 Corinthians 14:1; 2 Timothy 1:6-8). It also makes it easier for the Holy Spirit to speak to us if we are becoming prideful in such areas, as Paul had to do when he wrote to the Corinthians. In general, it is nearly impossible to function in this Christian life without a practical knowledge of the fear of the Lord.

1 Peter 5:8: "*Be sober, be vigilant; because your adversary, the devil, as a roaring lion, walketh about, seeking whom he may devour.*"

Chapter Five

The Traps

One might wonder what's the difference between a danger, as I titled the last chapter, from a trap? Frequently, we put ourselves in danger, simply from disobedience or ignorance. Dangers can be used by our enemy, satan.[10] But a trap is specifically laid to ruin or stop God's people. It is a historical fact that each older move of God persecutes the new move of God. This is one of the saddest realities we know of in church history. God is getting ready to move in such a way that we will see many different manifestations of the glory of God; almost making it look like there are many different revivals going on. But in fact, it is one continuous, end-time revival. Not only will God use those who have remained faithful, but He is getting ready to raise up a bunch of "nobodies" in the church.

Even typing that is odd to me since we as saints are never nobodies, just brothers and sisters we have not met yet. Nevertheless, many of these folks have been beat up and trashed by the traditional church. They don't seem to fit in. But God is raising them up, not to do to their brothers what was done to them, but to be a blessing and to heal this rift, once and for all. Not everyone will be happy by this reality, but there it is. In fact, I have always maintained and been clear

---

[10] As stated in the very beginning of this book, I refuse to capitalize our enemy's name. Call it silliness, lack of proper grammar or artistic license, I still refuse to do it.

Suddenly

that whatever God is getting ready to do, quite frequently the church resists. But God's voice to the face of the earth is not in silence.

As I mentioned in a previous chapter, God speaks to the face of the earth. The church should hear and obey. Whether we refuse to obey or agree to obey, the world also hears and tries to do it. Because they are not in a love relationship with Jesus and filled with the Spirit of God, they cannot maintain God's directive. Instead, or quite often, the devil gets in and throws his narrative into the mix. When this happens, he uses the lie. When we believe enough lies over and over, a stronghold develops in those areas.

Let's look to the book of Esther in the Old Testament for an example of a modern-day stronghold. The government that made the laws for the largest part of the earth in that day was Babylon. To say Babylon was sexually pure would be an abject lie. With an anointing of God upon Israel, most normal people in Babylon would not have hated their Jewish neighbors. It would have taken a spirit desiring control, power or sexual power— all akin to rape— in order to make a law to destroy God's people. Babylon found that ancestry inside Haman. He came from a long line of Agagites. This is about 800 years in time after Ruth finds favor with God and becomes King David's great-grandmother.

To understand why we are seeing something here that is not natural, but a lie within a stronghold belief, we only need to look at the Scriptures and study the history (1 Samuel 15). Agag was the king who reigned when Saul was instructed of the prophet/judge Samuel to enact Godly judgment over the Amalekites. In 1 Samuel 15:3, God's instructions were given at the mouth of the prophet Samuel: "Take the stronghold and utterly destroy all, leave nothing spared." Saul doesn't do this; he spares many of them, including King Agag.

In Verse 9, God reveals Saul's heart: "They were unwilling to destroy completely." Why? Because in their eyes this plunder was valuable, even though God said it wasn't valuable enough to Him to keep it alive a minute longer than it needed to be. To the casual observer,

The Traps

Saul's argument to the prophet in 1 Samuel 15:20-21, seems legitimate: they killed with the sword and brought back the best to be sacrificed. After all, Saul eludes in Verse 24, the people outnumber him, and they start taking the spoil; so Saul gives in. But a closer look at Saul's response in Verses 20 and 21, will show that he knew better.

The Hebrew word Samuel uses in his instructions to Saul is *charam*. It conveys the meaning of separating something for total destruction as incense to be consecrated to the Lord. In other words, destroy it swiftly and immediately so that you never see it again. With Saul repeating the same word used by Samuel in his instruction in 1 Samuel 15:3— he repeats it in 1 Samuel 15:15, 20-21— it shows that he understood the full implication of the word. Saul desired to control the situation and manipulate the outcome. The Lord looks on this as arrogance. Samuel declares Saul's rebellion is as witchcraft and stubbornness is as idolatry. The Hebrew literally translates like this: "Indeed, (like) a sin of diviners is rebellion, (like) the iniquity of terafim (household idols) a display of arrogance."

Let's put it in third millennial terms. When you think what God has given you isn't good enough or you feel you've got a better way, that's control. When God attempts to reveal your heart to you, but you've got theology behind a list of excuses for not obeying God, that's manipulation and a display of arrogance in God's eyes. In 1,000 plus BC[11] Israeli terms, Samuel calls it witchcraft and idolatry (rebellion and stubbornness).

Look, if you will, at Isaiah 5:18-24 and Isaiah 42:8. You will see that God refuses to compete with our rebellion and stubbornness. They are witchcraft and idolatry to Him. Yet, the amazing part of Saul's story is that God gave Saul twenty-one years to repent after pronouncing judgment in 1 Samuel 15:26-29. Some argue that this re-

---

[11] Some time periods in the Bible are approximations. Unless we have an outside source to compare with, as in the case of Queen Esther, we simply do not know exactly when something takes place. Some modern scholars say when God said to destroy all, it was a euphemism; everybody knew He didn't really mean it. I disagree.

Suddenly

prieve gave Ruth's great-grandson, King David, time to learn how to be a better king. Definitely so, but God's plans are as multifaceted as He is in glory. The desire for power, control and manipulation are all present and visible in today's governments.

You might say, what has this story got to do with Esther? Well, quite a few scholars believe this Haman, who desired to kill all living Jews during Queen Esther's time is the long distance relative of those whom Saul spared in Agag's bloodline. The Bible doesn't tell us stories and parables just to fill up the pages of the book.

Whether we like it or believe it, God will have His way; and, He has a way of recording it that can leave you a scoffer or a believer, depending upon what's in your heart. If what's in your heart is covered in layers of demonic and unbelieving strongholds, then that is what will come out. There are two places in Esther where we see the stronghold, or unnatural thought process. As mentioned before, most normal people in Babylon would have no quarrel with their neighbor Jews. If they did, as Hamon did here, they wouldn't have wanted to destroy a whole nationality of people, but the single person or neighbor giving them the problem.

We all know the story. Esther's cousin, Mordecai would not bow before Hamon. He wouldn't do so because He **feared the God** of Abraham, Isaac and Jacob; the same God we serve as Christians. Instead of punishing Mordecai for this insult, Hamon wants to destroy all of the people who were the same ancestry as Mordecai in all of the realms of Babylon (Esther 3:6). This desire also lends credence to the history of the bloodline in Haman. Samuel killed many Agagites and now Haman wants to wipe out every Jew.

Like Americans, the Babylonians had many different cultures in the nation. As long as the laws were obeyed, great grace was given to the different cultural traditions of their neighbors. To destroy a whole people group for the perceived insult of one man is absurd. We know it was absurd from another portion of Esther.

The Traps

After the edict is delivered and brought to the attention of the entire realm, the Bible states in Esther 3:15: "The posts went out, being hastened by the king's commandment, and the decree was given in Shushan the palace. And the king and Haman sat down to drink; but the city Shushan was perplexed." It was such an odd command that the whole city was confused or perplexed by it. While the city is in confusion, the king thinks nothing of it and sits down to drink.

When what you are doing makes no common sense, follows no science nor follows the directives or commandments of God, it is a demonic stronghold. In America today, we are following demonic strongholds. We neither follow science nor reality. The reality of the 2020 election is so fraught with fraud, that it's almost easy to find.[12] Yet, the media is telling you not just to ignore it, but if you dare view any of the evidence and then find it credible enough to post, you will become marginalized and persecuted if you say anything about the fraud.[13]

Big Tech, along with social media giants attempt, and pretty much do, control all political science speech. You will rarely, if ever hear or

---

[12] From a secular, tech world: < deepcapture.com > Here is a two hour video bringing proof on three levels that America went through the biggest coup in our history and that the democrat winner in 2020 is not the real president of the US. < https://ugetube.com/watch/mike-lindell-the-fll-documentary-absolute-truth-election-fraud-exposed-2-5-21_OVBbgwOthuRWzb4.html > These two videos have been removed consistently by big tech, so prayerfully the urls will be pertinent when you read this book. They have remained constant from 3 to 6 months, longer than any other video I have seen. Here is a concise article listing the merits of each case of fraud in 2020 and the inane reasons judges denied each one. Only in one case was it denied because it was brought beyond the allotted timeframe: < https://thefederalist.com/2021/03/11/courts-repeatedly-refused-to-consider-trumps-election-claims-on-the-merits/ > sites accessed 6/19/21.

[13] < https://www.breitbart.com/2020-election/2020/11/10/anti-trumpers-look-to-blacklist-trumps-election-lawyers-make-them-famous/ >< https://www.breitbart.com/2020-election/2020/11/13/under-pressure-trump-lawyers-quit-in-pennsylvania/ >< https://www.newsmax.com/us/cnn-cancel-culture-big-tech-censorship/2021/01/17/id/1006021/ > sites accessed 6/19/21.

see anything they don't like. Our ministry offends them regularly; so much so, that artwork depicting our Savior on the cross, or anything of a purely religious nature accompanying the American flag is routinely denied advertisement.[14] Conservative members of Congress are stopped from positions which may influence others simply because as private citizens they said or wrote something the communist Democrats didn't like.[15]

America was founded and has functioned, until recently, within a political science realm that is republican in nature. Those ideals promote free speech, religious freedom, as well as privacy rights and individual liberties. Denying a member of Congress their constituent's access to committee positions and denying free speech and religious speech to citizens tells me powerful groups are living in a demonic stronghold. It tells me that their thought structures have been captivated and their motivations will mean certain annihilation to those they believe do not think as they do.

Saints, if God does not show up for us, the enemy's desire is to take America captive and then swallow the church up as Haman tried to do to the Jews in Esther's time.[16] I don't think America is the devil's only target. He has garnered communist/socialists in many countries who desire to control the world with their ideologies. What we need desperately is our Kinsman Redeemer, Jesus. If He doesn't come to rescue us, time will be cut off: and this is the devil's desire. He knows a great revival is coming. He can't let the church get loose. He can't

---

[14] < https://nebula.wsimg.com/811ac00975c55c05dd54e1f9f01436d9?AccessKeyId=D1B765CBBC658EF49FE8&disposition=0&alloworigin=1 > see page 12. Accessed 6/19/21.

[15] < https://spectator.org/marjorie-taylor-greene-committee-assignments-file/ >< https://www.washingtonexaminer.com/news/gop-warns-democrats-marjorie-taylor-greene-punishment-spurs-revenge > sites accessed 6/19/21.

[16] < https://www.dailywire.com/news/report-dem-congressmen-to-offer-document-to-biden-championing-secularism-attacking-christian-nationalist-movement >< https://ifapray.org/blog/democrats-demand-biden-to-remove-re-educate-conservative-christians/ > sites accessed 6/19/21.

have us believing God's word that the preaching of the Gospel is accompanied by signs and wonders. He can't have us baptized in the Holy Ghost and fire with the manifest presence of God in glory flowing over our endeavors and lives. And most of all, he can't allow millions of people to be led to the Lord to become part of the army of God.

Suddenly

Joel 2:23: "Be glad then, ye children of Zion, and rejoice in the Lord your God: for he hath given you the former rain moderately, and he will cause to come down for you the rain, the former rain, and the latter rain in the first month..."

Joel 2:28-32: "And it shall come to pass afterward, that I will pour out my spirit upon all flesh; and your sons and your daughters shall prophesy, your old men shall dream dreams, your young men shall see visions: And also upon the servants and upon the handmaids in those days will I pour out my spirit. And I will shew wonders in the heavens and in the earth, blood, and fire, and pillars of smoke. The sun shall be turned into darkness, and the moon into blood, before the great and terrible day of the Lord come. And it shall come to pass, that whosoever shall call on the name of the Lord shall be delivered: for in Mount Zion and in Jerusalem shall be deliverance, as the Lord hath said, and in the remnant whom the Lord shall call."

Chapter Six

Revival Regardless

While many in the world fought a virus, I was in a rehab center with broken bones. I had fallen and was rushed to emergency surgery. I spent the better part of four months laying around doing nothing. I determined in my heart that if the devil thought he could get away with that kind of nonsense, I was going to make him miserable. Saint or sinner, devils were getting cast out and everyone was going to hear the word of the Lord. So, pretty much business as usual.

The next thing the Lord did was speak to me about what was going on in the world and America. The vision/dreams He gave me let me know exactly what was about to take place and why the virus was unleashed. Thereafter, He showed me more concerning what He wanted to accomplish with an end-time revival. Needless to say, I saw a lot of people in wheel chairs during my waking and sleeping hours with dreams from the Lord. He used that to show me how much he desires dry bones to LIVE! He is getting ready to speak this to the Earth. We who are listening must be in a mindset that says, "God in glory; we desire to see nothing more and we will receive nothing less." We must have a determination to see God in glory rest upon us and the environment around us.

As the body of Christ, we have one thing that gets in the way to all this awesome revival of God: rebellion. Rebellion in our past that has caused many different denominations; rebellion in our own hearts and rebellion right now within the blood-bought, Spirit-filled church of God, will stop any move of God. If we decided to come together and put aside all our nonsense, it would be like the Hebrew words *tamei* and *shaatnez*. The Lord used these words in the Old Testament to show us what combining Mosaic Law with salvation by faith in Jesus Christ would look like. I'd like us to see this combination's ultimate end. Let me quote from my first book:

"God stirs up controversy every time He sends prophets or comes to earth Himself. Frankly, I think He does this just to show us our strongholds. Biblical history has shown us that instead of dealing with our issues we shoot the messengers. Without exception, every Old Testament prophet, including Jesus, came on the scene to break up what scholars have called priest-craft. Priest-craft as a stronghold is similar in its negative connotation to witchcraft, but it is different. Priest-craft is a result of our debate with God's desire to do things His way when He arrives on the scene. When we as priests function by Jesus Christ, who is the Word, through the Holy Spirit we function as holy vessels."

"When we confuse our fleshly understanding with God's holy desires, or when we substitute a portion of what He says for what we desire in our carnality, then we function in priest-craft. Two Old Testament words better explain this concept. When you tell Christian people not to sin, often their attitude sounds like this: 'I don't smoke or chew or go with those who do. So I don't sin.' It is hard to convince some people that spiritual sin is the same as physical sin. Strongholds are those attitudes that we use as a shield of faith to protect us instead of God. Only His Word and His Spirit can be our shield of faith. When we substitute our own systems of protection for His Word and mix our own desires with the Holy Spirit's commands, we function in two different Hebrew words. They are *tamei* and *shaatnez*."

"*Tamei* is most often translated as 'tainted or polluted.' More modern scholars believe that the word *tamei* is best translated through the modern word radioactivity.[17] In other words, the environment around us becomes so charged by the radioactive toxicity of our sin that God leaves. Here is the subtlety of radioactivity: In and of itself it is not toxic. What makes it toxic is that it fools you, causing you to exchange the real for the fake. Radioactive chemicals such as Strontium 90 mimic calcium; Cesium 137 mimics potassium and Carbon 14 mimics nitrogen. Our bodies depend upon calcium and potassium for good health. Every plant that grows on our planet needs nitrogen. When the real calcium, potassium or nitrogen are not present our bodies will substitute whatever counterfeit they find that mimics the real to survive. Plants do the same thing."

"In fact, this acceptance of counterfeit minerals is so dangerous that even after a small amount of exposure, our bodies can begin preferring the substitute counterfeit instead of the real even when the real is available because the counterfeit becomes easier to assimilate. Now, think of this in spiritual terms and how easy it is for us to get ideas, thoughts and pretensions (2 Corinthians 10:4-5), that can exalt themselves over and above what God thinks or knows. Satan will always try to substitute his ways instead of what God wants. Isn't this what the antichrist is, an attempt at substitution for Jesus Christ?"

"*Shaatnez* has to do with mixing things in matters in which only God is allowed to mix things. Under the Old Covenant fields, crops, clothing and animals fell into this category. While the word *tamei* dealt more with the pollution of the sanctuary, vessels and people, *shaatnez* encompassed what and how people survived outside the temple. Mixing could only be accomplished as God deemed fit, not according to their individual human judgment."

"The Old Testament leaders and priests worked hard to keep up the appearance of following these laws— they didn't smoke or chew or go with those who do— but, the very attitudes that these words and laws would have prevented had they been obeyed in their hearts,

---

[17] Everett Fox, "The Five Books of Moses; The Schocken Bible, Volume 1" (Schocken Books, Inc., New York, 1995) pages 497, 498.

were attitudes they functioned in every day. They had so twisted Scripture by substituting their own interpretations of the Law that they found it easy to crucify Christ, thus creating a *tamei*, or polluted spiritual environment. They so mixed God with their own desires that for forty more years they didn't miss a heart beat, but kept the temple going as if Christ had never arrived on the scene. They mixed what they thought God wanted with what He was actually doing on Earth."[18]

What was the key reason Ruth, Naomi and Esther saw deliverance? It was their fear of God. Instead of mixing their desires with what God wanted, they did His will. What was Samuel's instruction to Saul? Don't do things your way, burn these items on the altar. In other words, your obedience is the sacrifice in the fear of the Lord. I had several words from the Lord after the 2020 election. One was the promise of the arrival of our Kinsman Redeemer to rescue us. We are now in such a situation as God's people that we certainly need to be rescued. Another is the reality that when God does show up, or when He arises, His enemies are scattered (Psalm 68:1-4).

The third word is that God is getting ready to cross the streams of revival. He is getting ready to do what only God can do: He is getting ready to mix it up and bring the fire and streams of revival together in one end-time revival harvest. This "mixing" or crossing can only be done by God, else it is tamei and shaatnez. I've been sensing this for a very long time. God has been giving me tidbits here and there as well as the Scriptures to go along with it.

One day a few weeks back, another intercessor connected to this ministry was sharing with me that the Lord told her He was restoring a Spirit of Truth back into this nation; in fact, back into the

---

[18] Meier, Christine. 2002 "Beyond Strongholds: Infiltration By The Glory of God." Creation House Press, Orlando, Florida. Pages 21-23. You can get a copy on this site. < ccm4www.org > In fact, we'll send you one free if you click on the "Contact" link. You must request the book by name. This only applies within the United States. Otherwise shipping as well as other charges will apply.

church. I was sharing with her my burden for the fear of the Lord and its connection to revival. As we compared notes, we were moved to go to Isaiah 11. Before we review the fear of the Lord, let's look at Isaiah 10:27 first: "And it shall come to pass in that day, that his burden shall be taken away from off thy shoulder, and his yoke from off thy neck, and the yoke shall be destroyed because of the anointing." We must be struck and challenged with the conviction that there is nothing for us to do but obey. When our obedience is a reality, His anointing destroys all "yokes."

2 Corinthians 10:1-6 (Italics mine): "Now I, Paul, appeal to you personally by the meekness and gentleness of Christ (I who am meek when present among you, but am full of courage toward you when away!) — now I ask that when I am present I may not have to be bold with the confidence that (I expect) I will dare to use against some who consider us to be behaving according to human standards. For though we live as human beings, we do not wage war according to human standards, for the weapons of our warfare are not human weapons, but are made powerful by God for tearing down strongholds. We tear down arguments and every arrogant obstacle that is raised up against the knowledge of God, and *we take every thought captive to make it obey Christ*. We are also ready to punish every act of disobedience, whenever your obedience is complete" (NET Bible).

The NET Bible gives the impression that it is the apostles who will punish every act of disobedience once we obey, but quite a few other translations, as well as the King James, give a more general idea. While the NET Bible is absolutely within the parameters of the Greek text, other translations bring the action back to the subject of the weapons being mighty through God to the pulling down of strongholds. The connection conceptualizes obedience with God's act of grace through salvation. The Greek word used by Paul for 'weapon' is *hoplon*. The definition is any tool or implement for preparing a thing; that would include our bodies, arms, weapons as well as instruments of any kind.

Suddenly

2 Corinthians 10:3-6: "For though we walk in the flesh, we do not war after the flesh: (For the weapons of our warfare are not carnal, but mighty through God to the pulling down of strong holds;) Casting down imaginations, and every high thing that exalts itself against the knowledge of God, and bringing into captivity every thought to the obedience of Christ; And having in a readiness to revenge all disobedience, when your obedience is fulfilled" (King James Version).

With that understanding, it is God who punishes the disobedience because we have decided to obey. Or, it is this very private, as well as public act of obedience which causes the effect of God's grace entering into the fray. In the Greek "the obedience" is a noun. It is more like a caption called *The Obedience of Christ*. It is salvation, accepting Jesus. It is awesome because this— what I call a caption or status— is the understanding of His right standing with God. This is what we see similarly in Isaiah 10, as well as Isaiah 11. So we see an impetus for obedience; namely, God's grace as well as an elders' ability to come to our aid. We will study Isaiah 11 shortly.

Going back to Isaiah 10, we see the theme of governments instituting unrighteous laws and stealing from the poor and widows. We see God promise to judge this, as the prophet talks about the remnant Jews from among God's people being sent back to the land. We read a similar description from our passage in Joel 2. This is the atmosphere or the newsworthy headlines of the day. Surely, our own headlines today display these characteristics. Israel was sent back to her own land in 1948. Governments today make laws that are simply unjust; while those with slave-like mentalities try to rule over God's people, telling them what to do and how to behave and what to think.

The word *yoke* used here means exactly that. Yokes were used to force animals into collars so that agricultural work could be achieved. It comes from a Hebrew word that means 'to act severely, deal with severely, make a fool of someone; to act or play the child; to thrust someone into wickedness.' Isn't that what an attempt to control all worldly governments through communism is? Communism is a tool or ideology used by the devil as a weapon to control God's people. One could replace it with socialism, fascism or any other religious or secular type of belief system which desires to remove God-given rights of liberty.

The Hebrew word for anointing, *shemen*, means fatness or oil and it comes from the word *shaman*. It is where many cultures get their understanding for their words denoting doctors who perform various aspects of healing. We have become a royal priesthood because of Christ's right standing with God. When we stand in Christ's righteousness, we stand in obedience. It is that simple. It is a status symbol! We don't have to be perfect or be a movie star. It does not matter how poor or rich or beautiful we are. We don't have to beg, borrow or steal. Once we have accepted Christ, his obedience or right standing— righteousness— is passed to us and we have revival. He wants to come in revival more than we can even know.

When we understand that all else in this world means captivity and the only thing that frees us is when God comes in yoke-busting anointing, we will get tenacious about revival. When we understand the meaning of obedience is to be in right-standing with Jesus, and trust that God will and can save us, He does (Romans 5:18-21). All we need to do is accept Christ's sacrifice. He has already paid the price for our redemption. He has rescued His people in the past, and certainly we see from the book of Revelation that He does it in the future. So let's connect what it is that God is telling us.

We who fear the Lord know that a great end-time harvest revival is coming. While the enemy thinks he can stop this through various forms of persecution, we know God is able as our Kinsman Redeemer to protect and deliver us. When God arises, His enemies scatter (Psalm 68:1). This end-time revival will produce such a change in our environments that even government will be affected to whatever extent we are serious about returning a Spirit of Truth back to our individual countries.

Suddenly

Because God desires a partnership with mankind, when we do our part, He has already done His part (grace) and it seems as if He suddenly comes to His temple. Even so, Come Lord Jesus.

Suddenly

Isaiah 11:1-2: "And there shall come forth a rod out of the stem of Jesse, and a Branch shall grow out of his roots: And the spirit of the LORD shall rest upon him, the spirit of wisdom and understanding, the spirit of counsel and might, the spirit of knowledge and of the fear of the LORD."

Chapter Seven

The Fear Of The Lord

Let's review: God is getting ready to remove yokes that have kept the church, as well as many on planet Earth bound. He's getting ready to do it as a result of the anointing breaking yokes or bondages. That anointing is coming because of what King Jesus brings to our proverbial tables.

As mentioned in the last chapter, accepting Christ's sacrifice is obedience. Obedience brings Him to our tables. The partnership that we make with Jesus is profound. As a result, the Holy Spirit always reveals Jesus, His presence and His anointing. And all that He is, comes with Him. Isaiah 11:3, is talking about Jesus coming in the fear of the Lord. Let me share the highlighted Verse 3a from the NET Bible: "He will take delight in obeying the Lord."

The **fear of the Lord** is more than a respect. It is that, but it is an adoration of respect and trust. Neither the King James Version or the NET Bible renders the sentence literally from the Hebrew. The sentence literally says, "And his smelling is in the fear of the Lord." Odd, you might say? Well, in Amos 5:21, we have the Hebrew tense of this word translated the same way. There, the prophet is talking about God no longer smelling with delight the Israelites' temple sacrifices during their festivals or meetings. Because this verse in Isaiah carries no incense or fire, many translators refuse to note it. The NET Bible does in its volume of notes.

Suddenly

The word *ruakh* (or as some transliterate the spelling *ruwach*), is where we get the word *breath* from. The tense of the word used here is 'to smell.' I believe it must be included in any understanding of the fear of the Lord. Why? Because Jesus is described as coming to save and deliver Israel. He is noted as successful because He literally gives delight to the Lord because of His healthy fear of the Father. It is as a sweet smell before God Almighty. It is as a burnt sacrifice on the altar of worship.

This is the connection we see from our three women, Naomi, Ruth and Esther. This is the desire Samuel tries to convey to Saul, to no avail. This is why Ruth's great grandson becomes a king in the lineage of Jesus. This very sacrifice will waft up to our High Priest, Jesus, and to His Father and our Father. True worship always brings God to our tables. When Father and Son "smell" this incense, it will bring them as fire on our altars; living sacrifices before the Lord (Romans 12:1-3). When Father smells this, He will tell Jesus, It Is Time!

This is one reason why we cannot "mix" or cross streams as we desire. As the fear of the Lord is heightened in all Christian camps, Jesus will come and ignite the anointing for the harvest. Many will realize the walls that divide us are not from God. As this prophetic, evangelistic movement goes forth across the blood-bought, Spirit-filled church, the streams will cross so it becomes one long, end-time harvest revival.

This is what the enemy is fighting to stop by weaponizing a virus. This is why a computer system was accessed by the Internet so tens of thousands of votes could be changed. God doesn't care what the enemy thinks he has gotten away with. God doesn't care who wants to sit behind a desk or what laws they pass to try to destroy the church. It will not succeed.

As the enemy is trying to institute a worldwide communistic system to entangle the people of the earth, God is coming as Kinsman Redeemer: the Deliverer of His people. As the enemy thinks he will destroy and confiscate the people and property of God, God is giving the world a revitalized America as truth in government.

Each nation has a truth and healing or destiny to fulfill for planet Earth. America is no different. She will move in the word of God as truth for a government by and for the people, ensconced in freedom and liberty. She will sing the praises of God from one generation of Americans to another. As the streams of revival cross, the *fear of the Lord* and the glory of the Lord will cover the earth as the waters cover the seas. His glory will prevail. The Lion of the Tribe of Judah will prevail.

It doesn't matter what social media or corporations or governments do to silence this word; God is greater and will amplify His word to every corner of the earth. How do I know that God can once again use America? I know Jesus doesn't need this country or that country to do anything. But I do know during this time that Jesus will pick the country who will make it all about what He wants to do and do what God desires. Like America did in 1776, this country will move in the fear and admonition of the Lord. While it will not be a political revival, politics will have no choice but to change. We will once again see God invade politics, as He did in 1776, and produce a place of comfort and rest for His presence among His people.

And Israel will see this and become jealous for her Elder Brother to return. But, I am getting ahead of myself. One day at a time, one step at a time until we, like Enoch and Elijah are not because God has taken us (Genesis 5:24; 2 Kings 2:11)!

I do get so excited to see many saved and set free that I almost forgot that we need to review more concerning the fear of the Lord. What I see in the Hebrew are concepts that seem out of sequence, but if we were to look at this in English, we would realize that the energy or momentum is revering the Lord. That jumping point produces the sacrifice that God "smells" and when God shows up, He destroys yokes with His anointing and brings with Him a wisdom we have no earthly understanding for.

Suddenly

We see this sequence: The Spirit rests, bringing the spirit of wisdom and understanding, the spirit of counsel and might, the spirit of knowledge. This produces correct judgment: "he shall not judge after the sight of his eyes, neither reprove after the hearing of his ears: But with righteousness shall he judge the poor, and reprove with equity for the meek of the earth: and he shall smite the earth: with the rod of his mouth, and with the breath of his lips shall he slay the wicked. And righteousness shall be the girdle of his loins, and faithfulness the girdle of his reins" (Isaiah 11:3b-5).

This is what the church has been sorely lacking: a quick understanding how to judge appropriately. We will study this penultimately. But for now, let's take a look at God's grace within a spirit of wisdom, understanding, counsel, might and knowledge.

Suddenly

Ezra 8:9: "*For the grace of God has appeared, bringing salvation to all people*" *(NET Bible).*

Ephesians 2:4-10: "*But God, who is rich in mercy, for his great love wherewith he loved us, Even when we were dead in sins, hath quickened us together with Christ, (by grace ye are saved;) And hath raised us up together, and made us sit together in heavenly places in Christ Jesus: That in the ages to come he might shew the exceeding riches of his grace in his kindness toward us through Christ Jesus. For by grace are ye saved through faith; and that not of yourselves: it is the gift of God: Not of works, lest any man should boast. For we are his workmanship, created in Christ Jesus unto good works, which God hath before ordained that we should walk in them.*"

Romans 2:4: "*Or despisest thou the riches of his goodness and forbearance and longsuffering; not knowing that the goodness of God leadeth thee to repentance?*"

Chapter Eight

The Grace Of God

Some might say that they don't see grace anywhere within the context of the fear of the Lord. Well, God's grace is all over His action to save us. Understanding the proper, grace-filled action involved in the fear of the Lord, saves us and extends the love language of the Holy Spirit to us. As we see from our Scriptures for this chapter, it is His grace that extends salvation to us. It was Jesus' action of sacrifice that enabled our redemption.

We have done nothing to earn this great gift. I have to ask the question: if it's by His grace salvation is offered, why do we mix something we have nothing to do with, and our own human endeavors? All we have done is said, Yes! So often I will have an opportunity to listen to many different Christians. Frequently, it sounds like a hand-wringing contest concerning how much sin or other inadequacy is in their lives. Without a doubt there will always be inadequacies in the lives of us human beings. What we must do is get over it. When sin is evident, we must repent before God, change our minds and get on with whatever He has told us to do.

One of the hardest lessons for me to accomplish was nothing. You read that right. Jesus has allowed me to share the Gospel, start a church, write books, preach, teach, disciple and generally speaking, see His bride cared for as the Spirit directed. There are great men and women of God who have done so much more. I never feel as if

Suddenly

I've done enough and that's because I haven't done a thing. It's been all HIM! I can't take credit for my lack of doing anything, any more than I can take credit for anything that has benefited our Lord. I can't compare myself to anyone else either, because our only comparison is JESUS! He is the one the apostles tell us to model (1 Corinthians 11:1; Ephesians 5:1-2; 1 John 3:2-3; 2 Corinthians 3:17-18).

I've had the opportunity to train many horses, dogs and cats. I will tell you one constant over various species, is a lack of learning when they are nervous or in fear of some kind. All mammals learn when they are at peace. Can they learn from a fearful situation? Thankfully, yes, they can. But I can tell you plainly, that whenever I'm trying to teach an animal something, I must teach it to trust me first and then produce reward for the behavior I'm looking for.

When we brought our broodmares home, one was pregnant and the other was too young. Eleven months later, we had a foal on the farm. As is the custom with horses, the younger mare became an aunt to the older mare's foal. They pastured together in the same field. We added another mare and another foal was born. I watched as the "aunt" taught the foals how to drink water from the trough for the first time; what grasses to eat and what to stay away from, and how to interact with other species.

One day as I was watching this dynamic, the oldest foal went to the fencing to grab ahold of it and chew it. Trust me when I tell you that this is behavior I don't want to see. As I took a step to try to stop it, I realized I couldn't reach him in time for any action I might take to be beneficial. If I shooed him away, he'd think I was playing. What happened next surprised me. His "aunt" took her head and slammed the foal's head ever so gently, but forcefully. I realized immediately why she stopped him. Back in the day, our wood-fence treatment was a black, tar-like compound that was quite toxic to bugs. Regular wood had little or no treatment at all and probably tasted just fine; but the outside fencing probably tasted horrible. Instinctively, she knew not to eat it and taught him not to as well.

The Grace Of God

The reason she was able to teach him at all was because he trusted her and understood her language. When we trust God and take Him at His word, we learn His language. This produces a healthy respect and awe for who He is and what He does. This is my best understanding when discussing the definition of the fear of the Lord. When we view God as this big meanie or as someone who requires constant adherence as well as stroking, we learn nothing. When we play lip service to Him in worship and prayer in church, we understand very little about Him and His grace.

When we realize that it is His goodness and love that even leads us to repent, we desire to repent. When we realize that it is because of His grace we are saved and given the gift of salvation; that we haven't earned it, nor can we earn it, we relax around Him and worship freely. When we realize our part is to do nothing but acknowledge our need and then receive, we then come boldly to His throne in prayer and we receive mercy in our time of need (Hebrews 4:16).

When Jesus tries to communicate with us and we are in a dynamic other than faithful grace, this produces confusion within us. Our love language of grace and faith becomes lacking. When we know how much He loves us, sending His only begotten Son to die for us, we begin a journey of learning a new language of grace. Grace is the unmerited favor of God. It is His divine enablement to accept Him as Lord and Savior. When He does give me a task, His divine enablement gives me the ability to do it. Yes, I must do something, but only that which He enables me and asks me to do; nothing more, and nothing less.

Paul addressed this from the salvation side of divine grace when speaking to the churches. Since he singlehandedly wrote almost half of the New Testament, and started many of those churches he wrote to, no one can say he was lazy. Instead, he understood this dynamic of grace involved with our faith. He was succinct to the Galatians:

"O foolish Galatians, who hath bewitched you, that ye should not obey the truth, before whose eyes Jesus Christ hath been evidently set forth, crucified among you? This only would I learn of you, Received ye the Spirit by the works of the law, or by the hearing of faith? Are ye so foolish? Having begun in the Spirit, are ye now made perfect by the flesh" (Galatians 3:1-3)?

Over many years I have had a multitude of intercessors come to our ministry wanting to learn about prophetic ministry. In every case I am encouraged by the Holy Spirit to enlist Him in the discipleship. First, we make sure they are not under the Law. The Law, you say? How awful; who would be involved with that over 2,000 years later? Well, almost every church I've heard of. It no longer involves us going to a temple to sacrifice sweet little farm animals. This new seduction is far more sinister.

I realized it almost happened to me. We start off gloriously saved and going on our way with Jesus; when all of a sudden our pastor innocently enough asks us to do something. Of course we comply; these are our pastors, after all. Over time, more duties are given to us and we eventually get opportunities to take care of the sheep. We worry for them and are grieved when they grieve and become joyful when they are joyful. There is nothing wrong with that. Until one day the Holy Spirit comes to you and says, "You know, it's not your job to take care of everyone. I'm able to take care of them Myself!"

When I heard Him say that, I was stunned. It stopped me in my tracks. You see, every church feels it has more to accomplish than it can. There is work upon work to do. Some of it is seeing souls saved. Quite often, though, it is a new conference or a new luncheon or a new Bible study. I've got to go to the store and get supplies and cookies and whatever else. Maybe it's the things needed for the children for children's church or Sunday school. But before you know it, you are worked to death. And, before you realize it, you're heading down a slippery slope of needing to feel accepted by what you are doing instead of by reason of the cross of Christ.

I was arrested by the Holy Spirit long before I hit that point. But many don't allow the word to infuse their hearts. Many don't sit before the Lord to hear what it is that the Spirit is saying to the churches. When we sit with Jesus, we avoid these pitfalls. Let me share another important step we can take to help us avoid that trap.

We must hear from God and then we must understand His language of grace. God speaks to me often, and I have to confess, quite often I have no idea what He means or what I'm supposed to do. I've taken great comfort in knowing that this is the Creator of the Universe we're talking about here. If I understood everything He was saying, I'm not sure it would really be God who was speaking to me. When I relax, and sit before Him with the word or in song, in praise and worship, I find rest and peace and faith swelling up within me.

Frequently after such time spent with Him, I will instantly know what it was that the Spirit was trying to say to me. Each one of us must take time and learn how He speaks with us. This is all part and parcel in understanding the fear of the Lord. If you do not respect someone, or you do not care what someone thinks or knows, you will not spend time nor desire to spend time with them. I hear these words quite often when sharing with people along this topic: "I never hear from God; that's just me." That is an opinion based on false facts.

The devil will always tell us that God is just too busy or can't talk to us for some other reason. We must press in. We must take time and energy to do this. For some of us it will take days; for others weeks; for others, months. There are those folks where it will take years. Please take heart; God wants to speak with us. Daniel fasted twenty-one days in order to receive a visitor from the throne of God. When the angel of the Lord did show up, Daniel was told that he had been held up by satanic forces over the regions of countries (Daniel 10:11-14).

This is why I make mention of countries and governments in this book. The religious would tell you that we don't need to talk about politics. Saints, let me say plainly, while God can institute kings (Daniel 2:20-21); we, the people, must make our choices when it

Suddenly

comes to what governs us (Daniel 2:22-24). I make mention of this simply because we don't know what is going on in the heavens. We don't know what is holding up an answer or why we don't always hear what we want to hear. None of that should be used as an excuse to forego sitting before the Lord to listen.

It should also not be used as an excuse as to why we can't or won't go and do what it is the Lord has graced and called us to do. We are under a New Covenant. Certainly, over some regions of this world our enemy has hindered the Gospel. Nevertheless, when our Lord gives us a commission, that means He goes with us to do what He has called us to do (Matthew 28:18-20; Mark 16:15-20). We have something Old Testament saints did not have. We have the blood of Jesus, the Name of Jesus as well as the indwelling Holy Spirit. The word He gives us to speak— His word in our mouth— is as powerful as if He said it. When we go to do what Jesus tells us to do, we go under an open heaven. The devil is an interloper with no rights over us, unless we give it to him; and, that's the catch. He can have nothing on us. He had nothing on Jesus (John 14:30-31).

As we reviewed already, the fear of the Lord is like a sweet smell before Him. Imagine being absolutely starved and pulling in your driveway. All of a sudden you smell your favorite meal cooking. I dare say, you will jump from the car and run in the house. You may already know what's cooking, but you ask anyway. A conversation ensues and boom! Before you know it, you're eating and satisfied. This is what it is like when we have the understanding of the fear of the Lord mixed with a true understanding of His grace towards and for us. It's like Jesus sends whatever He must to our tables to facilitate the communication. Trust, grace-filled faith, time in reading His word and time in worship all bring us closer to the One who loves us and has captured our attention.

This is why we see the spirit of wisdom and understanding, the spirit of counsel and might, the spirit of knowledge accompanied by the understanding of the fear of the Lord. I've mentioned this before but it deserves repeating: When God shows up, all of Him shows up with

The Grace Of God

Him. It's a simple concept but one we forget so often. He realizes we are but dust and that He is simply too much of a good thing if He showed up full force. So He comes among us lightly. Even then, He overpowers us.

I've heard ministers call it being smashed in the presence of God. I've had my husband carry me in from the car after many church meetings where the presence of Almighty God overpowered us. How he was able to drive, I'll never know. But this is what it's like when the *suddenly* of revival arrives. Let's look at what is termed the sevenfold Spirit of God.

Suddenly

John 16:13-15: "*Howbeit when he, the Spirit of truth, is come, he will guide you into all truth: for he shall not speak of himself; but whatsoever he shall hear, that shall he speak: and he will shew you things to come. He shall glorify me: for he shall receive of mine, and shall shew it unto you. All things that the Father hath are mine: therefore said I, that he shall take of mine, and shall shew it unto you.*"

Chapter Nine

The Seven-Fold Spirit Of God

Teaching on this subject can hale from the silly to the sublime. I may be taking the middle road for some, but I choose to stand on what I see from the canon of Scripture. Most of what's out there from either side of the spectrum has to do with Second Temple Jewish theology peripheral to our topic.[19] Since I am no scholar on the peripherals or Second Temple theology, I choose to go no further than what the Bible lays out specifically. Like others, I do not see that there are seven spirits, but seven attributes to the Holy Spirit's nature. Similarly, I believe the number seven speaks to the complete picture we are seeing of the Spirit of God in each portion of Scripture He is revealed to us within the Bible.

I'm not particularly worried I may miss something from God theologically on this subject. First, that's because I don't believe we have to know everything theologically in order for God to come in revival. We don't need to know everything for us to be witnesses for Christ in order to see many led to our Lord. Secondly, when Jesus wants us to know something, He will teach us because the Holy Spirit guides us into all truth.

---

[19] As an example, here is a book: "Reversing Hermon: Enoch, the Watchers, and the Forgotten Mission of Jesus Christ." 2017. Copyright © Michael S. Heiser. United States

Third, we do have quite a bit from the canon of Scripture to go on in order to understand when God moves among us suddenly in revival. From Isaiah 11, we have reviewed the Spirit of God, the fear of the Lord, the spirit of wisdom and understanding, the spirit of counsel and might, the spirit of knowledge. I've mentioned my nugget that we discovered while looking at the Hebrew in Isaiah of a central point in this list. Isaiah is talking about Messiah. From our understanding as Christians, that can be none other than Jesus Christ. As we read from Isaiah, the fear of the Lord becomes like incense or a holy offering of sacrifice which invites God to our proverbial tables.

As Christians, we are quite fortunate to have cross-referenced Scriptures from John's Gospel, the book of Revelation and the epistle the Apostle Paul sent to Corinth. There are other scriptural references from many other biblical passages. For our purpose here, let's keep it simple and review John 14:16-26; 15:26-27; 16:7-15; Revelation 1:4; 3:1; 4:5 and 5:6. When you have finished reading those passages, head on over to 1 Corinthians 2:10-15, as well as Galatians 5:22-26.

When God shows up, everything that He is shows up with Him. You can't separate our God into different parts. Yes, He is the Almighty and He is Sovereign. This never changes; but, He is also the Triune God, in an eternal context of functioning within an interdependent and mutually beneficial relationship of Father, Son and Holy Spirit. You can't separate that, but you can highlight different aspects of who He is.

He is The Father, a good Father; parenting us and coming to our aid and rescue in times of need. He is The Son, our Elder Brother and Lord, saving us, redeeming us and giving us entry into a whole new family identity. He is The Holy Spirit, leading us and guiding us into all Truth. Any theology class would help students understand the different aspects of who God is. To make this topic more voluminous and intense, because they are One, they move in time and space similarly as One, but they can do so separately.

The Seven-Fold Spirit Of God

We know from Scripture when Jesus was no longer walking the earth, He promised to send the Comforter, the Holy Spirit (see the above referenced passages from John 14, 15 and 16). So we know Jesus is not on the earth any longer in corporeal form; the Holy Spirit is here. The Holy Spirit resides within believers on the earth.

He can move as swift as lightning (2 Samuel 22:13; Psalm 29:7; Daniel 10:6; Hosea 6:5; Matthew 24:27; Revelation 4:5). We know He speaks outside of time and space, yet can speak time and space into existence and function within time and space. "Remember the former things of old: for I am God, and there is none else; I am God, and there is none like me, Declaring the end from the beginning, and from ancient times the things that are not yet done, saying, My counsel shall stand, and I will do all my pleasure" (Isaiah 46:9-10).

So when we are looking at passages explaining the seven aspects or characteristics of the Spirit of God, it will take a bit more than a chapter in a book. This book is not meant as that study. What I would like to do is look at the Hebrew words used to define these characteristics within the Spirit of God and connect them to God coming amongst us in all-consuming glory. Since I am challenging us with becoming like Christ, I believe we will need to become more like the Christ we see prophesied by Isaiah. Or, to put it more particularly, to take our rest in the Holy Spirit by allowing the same spiritual reality to consume us that consumed Messiah, reflected in Isaiah 11.

I've already mentioned that I believe when the whole body of Christ functions in the fear of the Lord, that Father will receive this desire as incense. He will say, It is time; and cross the streams of various denominational revivals we have previously seen. This will usher us into an end-time revival. So it behooves us to understand the words. The Spirit of the Lord, "Ruakh" is defined as breath, wind, spirit. It is the same word used in Verse 3, but its tense is different. Verse 3 is translated as mind, or understanding in the King James, but should be translated as *smell*. We highlighted that in Chapter Seven. In Verse 2, it can be read as 'Breath of YHVH' (or Yahveh/Jehovah).

Suddenly

The word wisdom is used 149 times in the Bible and it is similarly used here. The word for understanding is different from *ruakh*, used in Verse 3. The Hebrew *biynah*, describes discernment and knowledge, but has an additional impetus as an action. The word counsel, *etsah*, carries with it a purpose. It comes from a primitive word to give advice and to consult together or conspire. While the primitive root can describe a condition of starting trouble, *etsah* simply carries the purpose of giving advice.

Ghbuwrah, or a spirit of might also has an action of strength and valor, bravery or mighty deeds connected to it. *Da'ath*, the Hebrew word used here for knowledge, comes from a primitive root which means to see as a seer or to perceive as one. *Da'ath* leans toward perception, knowledge, cunning, skill and understanding.

Except for the tense of the word used in Isaiah for breath as smelling, there is nothing unusual about these words. I believe that's because these concepts should be our everyday experience with the Spirit of God. What makes the passage intense is what the concepts connect to; namely, Messiah's fear of the Lord in understanding, wisdom, knowledge, counsel, might and knowledge in passing judgment. We will look at this more in-depth shortly. For now though, we need to connect this to the Spirit's work among the churches.

When we connect what we see in Isaiah 11, to the New Testament's passages, we begin to understand how the Holy Spirit is working among us to bring about a bride who can judge appropriately and in Godly authority. I believe this to be one manifestation of the Holy Spirit that we will see in any end-time revival. While it is exciting to experience God's manifest presence in revival meetings, I feel as if we sometimes look for nothing else but falling down, shaking, crying or laughter. From personal experience I can tell you that is awesome; but it is so far from experiencing the fullness of the Holy Spirit in power.

When we connect the fear of the Lord— understanding, wisdom, knowledge, counsel, might— and how we hear the Holy Spirit of

The Seven-Fold Spirit Of God

God speak to us in our daily lives, we open doors to see all God has promised us and promised to do for the bride of Christ. Nothing becomes impossible to us. This is the awesome power of the Holy Spirit operating in our midst, wherever we are standing, whether in our homes, churches, on a street or work. These are all the places we can experience His revival as we operate in the fullness of the seven-fold Spirit of God.

In fact, the Scripture that tells us all things are possible to him who believes (Mark 9:23), comes from a discourse between a father and Jesus. The man was obviously at his last hope, having dealt with a demon that kept throwing his child from fire to water trying to kill him. You can hear the unbelief in his voice when he tells Jesus what is going on and says, "If you can do anything, have pity on us." It elicits the famous verse so many quote. It's the man's next request, along with the reaction of the crowd that releases the miracle: "And straightway the father of the child cried out, and said with tears, 'Lord, I believe; help thou mine unbelief.' "

When we receive by faith the whole truth of salvation in Jesus Christ, accepting Him by faith and confessing Him with our mouths, we enter into grace; a divine enablement to receive all that Christ has for us. The Spirit of God comes to reside in us. This, in and of itself produces a healthy fear of the Lord which ushers in wisdom to escape a problem and wisdom to receive what He has for us; wisdom to live this life in the here and now. We receive understanding for that which concerns us. We become counseled by the Holy Spirit who resides in us and we receive strength or might to accomplish.

This father of a demon possessed child received the wisdom to go to Jesus in the first place. Only the Spirit can draw us in this regard. Once he did that, he received the strength or might to admit his lack of faith. In some folks it takes courage to admit a lack in character, or a need in our dispositions. He also received the understanding necessary for his situation in order to see his child delivered. When we receive the Savior, we receive everything the Spirit of God can offer us.

Suddenly

This produces a knowledge that the world, or worldly vision does not have. It produces a knowledge, a faith and a strength to receive revelation and deliverance. We function in accurate assessment or judgment for everyday life. This is what we receive of the seven-fold manifest Spirit of God. He counsels us. This is the Holy Spirit: the one who raised Jesus from the dead. Romans 8:11: "But if the Spirit of him that raised up Jesus from the dead dwell in you, he that raised up Christ from the dead shall also quicken your mortal bodies by his Spirit that dwelleth in you."

Thirty-five plus years ago I was listening to one of our former pastors preach a sermon challenging us from Romans 8. While he was preaching, the Holy Spirit said to me, "You know, you don't have to wait for all of this to be in the future after you die. You can live like this now." I was a younger believer and wanted to test what I was hearing. I went to Romans 8 and started a study. I was flabbergasted. While resurrection from the dead is, of course, after death, much of Romans 8 is for us in the here and now.

The Holy Spirit resides in us, and on an everyday basis we can live by and through Him. We don't have to live after the Law any more but after the grace He gifts for us. This is the only way for the church to thrive. The only way for any church to survive or any Christian to live is by resting in what Jesus did, and doing only that which the Holy Spirit enables us to do; nothing more and nothing less.

That means we are going to experience, up close and personally the Spirit of God, the fear of the Lord, His wisdom, understanding, knowledge, might and counsel. It was not long after that study the Spirit took me through 1 Corinthians, Ephesians and other epistles. From there I realized the Holy Spirit was telling me we are a human never before seen on this planet. We are totally a new creation. We are the super heroes. Rather than wait for the future, let's get started today while we can hear His voice for the face of the earth. This becomes revival in our own hearts on an everyday basis.

Suddenly

Isaiah 11:3-5: "And shall make him of quick understanding in the fear of the LORD: and he shall not judge after the sight of his eyes, neither reprove after the hearing of his ears: But with righteousness shall he judge the poor, and reprove with equity for the meek of the earth: and he shall smite the earth: with the rod of his mouth, and with the breath of his lips shall he slay the wicked. And righteousness shall be the girdle of his loins, and faithfulness the girdle of his reins."

Chapter Ten

True Judgment

Our highlighted verses of Scripture for this chapter are Isaiah 11:3-5. When most ministers preach on these verses, the end-times and possibly the action of a new heaven and earth are shared. I'd like us to view a different aspect from these passages. Whenever the subject of God's judgment comes up, the grace crowd frowns and the religious crowd salivates. One, thinking I'm going to start beating people up and the other taking joy in the thought that I'm finally going to tell those sinners how inadequate and sinful they are. I'm not going to do either. Hopefully, the chapter on God's grace helped you to understand that grace has nothing to do with beating people up or puffing them up. If that's the case with true grace, it's also true for correct judgment related to God.

I'd like to highlight my definitions of judgment. The first would be how we judge or perceive God. The second would be how we judge each other. The third would be how God judges us or sees us, and the last would be how God in authority must judge what goes on in this world and the world to come. Some would say my definitions are incorrect because when we discuss God's judgment we must discuss only end-time events and not assessments made in this lifetime on earth. I disagree and that's because of what we see in Isaiah as well as Revelation as it pertains to the churches and the Spirit of God.

Suddenly

Looking at our passages in Isaiah where we read of the Spirit of the Lord, we see that Messiah is made to be "of quick understanding in the fear of the Lord: and he shall not judge after the sight of his eyes, neither reprove after the hearing of his ears: But with righteousness shall he judge the poor, and reprove with equity for the meek of the earth: and he shall smite the earth: with the rod of his mouth, and with the breath of his lips shall he slay the wicked. And righteousness shall be the girdle of his loins, and faithfulness the girdle of his reins" (Isaiah 11:3-5).

"John to the seven churches which are in Asia: Grace be unto you, and peace, from him which is, and which was, and which is to come; and from the seven Spirits which are before his throne" (Revelation 1:4). "And unto the angel of the church in Sardis write; These things saith he that hath the seven Spirits of God, and the seven stars; I know thy works, that thou hast a name that thou livest, and art dead" (Revelation 3:1). "And out of the throne proceeded lightnings and thunderings and voices: and there were seven lamps of fire burning before the throne, which are the seven Spirits of God" (Revelation 4:5). "And I beheld, and, lo, in the midst of the throne and of the four beasts, and in the midst of the elders, stood a Lamb as it had been slain, having seven horns and seven eyes, which are the seven Spirits of God sent forth into all the earth" (Revelation 5:6).

Judgment Defined and Exposed

We've already connected the Spirit of God in Isaiah to the same Spirit of God in the book of Revelation, and connected the self-same Holy Spirit to the seven-fold manifest presence of God. We see He, along with Jesus Christ speaks to the churches (1:4). We see He judges the churches; namely, if He judges one, He obviously can judge the others (3:1). We see He comes out of the throne of God, which is a place of occupation, denoting authority, creation, power, judgment and Being. In other words, He Is, and He is a rewarder of those who diligently seek Him (see Revelation 4:5, as well as Hebrews 11:6).

True Judgment

This connection speaks of relationship, and specifically human relationship to the Living God. If that connection weren't enough, we see it clearly mentioned that in the midst of the throne were the elders of the church and the Lamb of God and the seven-fold manifest Spirit of God (5:6). While no true child of God would ever presume such proximity to the throne of God, we don't have to fear an attitude of usurpation, haughtiness and rebellion since the Bible itself tells us that we are seated in heavenly places with Christ Jesus (Ephesians 2:6). There it is told us that it is the infinite grace of our God to display such actions of grace and kindness towards us for eternity (Ephesians 2:4-7).

He is an Awesome God! His throne speaks of authority, relationship, power and judgment. Since we are in close relationship to our heavenly Father and Jesus Christ, His only begotten Son and the Holy Spirit, we know we must also learn how to judge appropriately.

This is what Adam neglected to learn. This is what Jesus has come back to restore to us: mankind's sovereignty for planet Earth, his sovereign relationship as an emissary of the Almighty to the rest of God's created beings as well as the sovereign supernatural nature of how Adam and Eve were created. All of this was lost at the Fall. If we cannot even judge (assess) one another correctly, how shall we learn how God judges us? If we cannot even understand how His creation functions, how shall we judge angels appropriately (1 Corinthians 6:3-5; 11:29-33)?

I wish I could write a whole book on the proper assessment or nature of Godly judgment. Obviously, I cannot; I need an extra lifetime to learn more on this topic myself! I can only bring us small nuggets I found in some of the passages I've mentioned. From Isaiah, we see Messiah has moved in the appropriate fear of the Lord, judging God as worthy, and giving Him the respect due. This is received by Father, God as a sacrifice and incense before His throne. This is the first place we must start.

Suddenly

Too often preachers and ministers give the impression God is some big butcher in heaven getting ready to whack each wrong thought or action from us. If this were the case, no human would be able to remain alive in our world. Thankfully, this is not God. It was not easy for Jesus to display God as Father to the Jewish people of His day. For them, God had to be appeased with the blood of bulls and goats and birds; offerings from the field had to be made consistently. Their wrong assessment of God would always hamper their relationship with Him.

There is a reason the religious leaders made the accusation of Jesus and His followers as eaters, drinkers and partiers, while John's followers were holy people who fasted. They couldn't understand it. The joy and celebratory like attitude Jesus had when it came to a relationship with mankind as Elder Brother is because of Jesus' relationship to the Almighty as Father and Son. Jesus had been away from the rest of the family for a while since He hadn't been introduced to us yet until He took on human flesh. In fact, we couldn't be real family until He was sacrificed and we made the choice to accept His Passion.

Imagine not seeing loved ones for a lengthy period of time. Since this crazy lockdown, many of you don't need to imagine it. What did you do once you got a chance to see them again? Did you jump with excitement and take out the good family china to feed them on? Did you have a party? Did you hug them and give kisses of familial joy? Did those crazy aunts and uncles pinch those baby cheeks? Did some of the youngsters walk away with slobbery faces? Ha, of course we did!

The Jewish religious leaders of Jesus' day had never seen such a display toward God as family among their fellow Jews. While the theology of God as Father wasn't unheard of, the reality was not within their experience. Some rabbis did call the Holy Spirit the bat kohl, or "daughter voice," but an involved understanding of God as Father was yet to come. Jesus would have to model that for them and us.

We are in just the opposite dynamic. We view God as our Father; yet, our own earthly fathers can cloud our heavenly perception. We also view our ministers similarly thus making it sometimes impossible for a woman to pastor, while it puts men on pedestals as if they were movie stars. Heaven help us when we do begin to function with signs and wonders following the preaching of the Gospel. None of this helps the body of Christ moving forward in taking the earth for Jesus as the early church did.

Just as the religious leaders of Jesus' day had a hard time relating to Jesus, there are many religious leaders of today who have a hard time relating to those free spirits within the body of Christ. We don't always assess people correctly, thus judging what we don't know or understand. This is why it is paramount to function in and with the Holy Spirit. It would do all of us a world of good to hold off on judging folks until the Holy Spirit has spoken with us. At the very least as leaders, we must pray for the sheep God sends our way and ask the Great Shepherd how He wants His sheep cared for.

Present-Day Body Assessment

Before we look at our last categories of judgment, I'd like to mention the reality of when sheep need to move on to another church. Quite often, this brings consternation to many within the congregation, as well as some in leadership. We must always remember we are under-shepherds. The sheep already have a Great High Shepherd. If He has decided that they must move on, we must let them go, only blessing them on their way to where Jesus is sending them.

In my opinion, there are only two questions which must be asked. One, "Are you leaving because of someone in leadership? Has anyone in leadership, including myself harmed you or upset you in any way? Has something else taken place which has concerned you?" And the second is, "Can we send you off with a blessing so you go to your next assignment by our Savior with gratitude and in peace?"

Suddenly

I realize in large congregations the senior pastors can hardly know everyone coming in and out. Of course, this is why they have many staff pastors. As senior pastors, letting the staff know you will be asking these questions can also weed out those in error. It lets them know the kind of care expected to be given our family members.

If we don't ask these questions, I don't believe we are genuine shepherds. Just assuming we're perfect or nothing has taken place which genuinely must be addressed, in my opinion, means we are in denial to our own humanity. If we don't ask to bless our brothers and sisters with prayer as they go to wherever Jesus sends them, means we may have a latent attitude of hostility toward them, or some other negative attitude within us. Both are dangerous in leadership within the body of Christ.

The Bloodline

Next, I would like to look at God's judgment of mankind through the bloodline. To understand that, we only need to see how He views Jesus. That's because it is through the blood of Christ that Father God sees us. This is why we must accept Christ as Lord and Savior. It is only through His sacrifice that we can be saved. These passages in Ephesians say it plainly. I have underlined each concept or viewpoint of assessment. I also underlined all these passages to show you plainly on paper how God views us. This, from only three short chapters; obviously, there is the whole Bible! We receive these things from Father and are viewed by Him through the light of Jesus:

"<u>Grace</u> be to you, and <u>peace, from God our Father, and from the Lord Jesus Christ.</u> Blessed be the God and Father of our Lord Jesus Christ, who hath <u>blessed us with all spiritual blessings in heavenly places in Christ:</u> According as he hath <u>chosen us</u> in him before the foundation of the world, that <u>we should be holy and without blame before him in love:</u> Having <u>predestinated us unto the adoption of children by Jesus Christ to himself,</u> according to the good pleasure of his will, To the praise of the glory of his grace, wherein he hath <u>made us accepted in the beloved</u>" (Ephesians 1:2-6).

True Judgment

"Wherein he hath <u>abounded toward us in all wisdom and prudence;</u> Having <u>made known unto us the mystery of his will,</u> according to his <u>good pleasure which he hath purposed in himself</u>: That in the dispensation of the fulness of times he might <u>gather together in one all things in Christ,</u> both which are in heaven, and which are on earth; even in him: In whom also we have <u>obtained an inheritance,</u> being <u>predestinated according to the purpose of him who worketh all things after the counsel of his own will</u> (Ephesians 1:8-11)."

"In whom ye also trusted, after that ye heard the word of truth, the gospel of your salvation: in whom also after that <u>ye believed, ye were sealed with that holy Spirit of promise, Which is the earnest of our inheritance</u> until the redemption of the purchased possession, unto the praise of his glory (Ephesians 1:13-14)."

"That the God of our Lord Jesus Christ, the Father of glory, may <u>give unto you the spirit of wisdom and revelation in the knowledge of him: The eyes of your understanding being enlightened; that ye may know what is the hope of his calling, and what the riches of the glory of his inheritance in the saints,</u> And what is the <u>exceeding greatness of his power to us-ward</u> who believe, according to <u>the working of his mighty power</u> (Ephesians 1:17-19)."

"But God, who is rich in mercy, for his <u>great love wherewith he loved us,</u> Even when we were dead in sins, <u>hath quickened us together with Christ, (by grace ye are saved;) And hath raised us up together, and made us sit together in heavenly places in Christ Jesus:</u> That in the ages to come he might <u>shew the exceeding riches of his grace in his kindness toward us through Christ Jesus.</u> For by grace are ye saved through faith; and that not of yourselves: it is <u>the gift of God</u> (Ephesians 2:4-8)."

"For we are <u>his workmanship, created in Christ Jesus unto good works,</u> which God hath before ordained that we should walk in them" (2:10). "But now in Christ Jesus ye who sometimes were far off <u>are made nigh</u> by the blood of Christ. For he <u>is our peace, who hath made both one, and hath broken down the middle wall of partition</u>

between us" (2:13-14). "For through him we both <u>have access by one Spirit unto the Father.</u> Now therefore ye are <u>no more strangers and foreigners, but fellow citizens with the saints, and of the household of God"</u> (2:18-19). "In whom ye also are <u>builded together for an habitation of God through the Spirit</u> (2:21)."

"That he would <u>grant you, according to the riches of his glory, to be strengthened with might by his Spirit in the inner man;</u> That Christ may <u>dwell in your hearts by faith</u>; that ye, <u>being rooted and grounded in love, May be able to comprehend with all saints what is the breadth, and length, and depth, and height; And to know the love of Christ, which passeth knowledge, that ye might be filled with all the fulness of God</u> (Ephesians 3:16-19)."

In the beginning of Ephesians 3, Paul lets them know that God called him to be the apostle to the Gentiles. God called him to preach what was revealed to him concerning the mystery of Christ. Paul said that we, as God's children would benefit through his teaching, revelation, and prayers for us. One could accurately say that it is because of how Father God views us through the blood of Christ that He called Paul, and we benefited from his calling.

In Ephesians 4, along the lines of the previous train of thought, we also see Paul expound on the five-fold ministry gifts of apostle, prophet, evangelist, pastor and teacher. These people, called by our Lord, are gifts to His body, the bride of Christ. Their assignment is to bring the whole body into maturity, even the fullness seen in the Head, which is Christ (Ephesians 4:15). It could be easily argued that we even have such people seen within the body as gifts because of how Father views Jesus, knowing that the body needs such gifts.

Some folks get angry when Christians say this, but if humans do not accept Christ's sacrifice for their sin, then those humans must pay for their own sin by following the Mosaic Law. I can tell you after a review of the Mosaic Law, that it is impossible to do that. Nevertheless, if you feel you want to do that, far be it from me to try to stop you.

True Judgment

You should know that if God does not see the blood of Christ on you as a human, then His judgment is already declared on those who do not have their sin paid for. God does not want humans going to the Lake of Fire for eternity since it was built for the devil and those who follow him. But if He is not able to judge you through Christ's blood, then that will be where those humans will be sent. This is end-time judgment. It is called the Great White Throne Judgment seen in Revelation 20:11-15.

There is one last category of judgment I would like to discuss. Early on in the book of Acts we see where a husband and wife came to church and lied to the elders about what they gave in monetary donation to the congregation. The elders were clear that they had not lied to man, but to God. Judgment fell upon them in the form of immediate death. In the next chapter I'd like to explore different aspects of what I believe will be an increase in the body of Christ moving in Godly authority.

Many church folk would like to just pronounce judgment on people and be done with it. But the body cannot do what the Head does not allow. With that in mind, let's look at what I believe we will see within various revival camps in the future concerning proclamatory, Godly judgment and how the body of Christ in revival functions.

Suddenly

Daniel 7:21-22: "I beheld, and the same horn made war with the saints, and prevailed against them; Until the Ancient of days came, and judgment was given to the saints of the most High; and the time came that the saints possessed the kingdom."

Chapter Eleven

Possessing The Kingdom

There is a place in time when God's people will be able to judge and rule as God originally designed Adam and Eve to do for the planet and the creation on it. The kingdom of God is much bigger than a mere nation or a planet. Nevertheless, God started Adam and Eve's learning process on a planet that had nations. One might say these were their baby steps or God's kindergarten class for sovereign immortals. Adam and Eve were designed to act as sovereigns and judge properly in matters relating to the creation and the planet. They were then to make that representation to the Council in heaven, and then represent the Council in heaven back to the creation here on earth. This was lost at the Fall. Specialized gifts were necessary for that job and we lost the ability to access those gifts as well.

So much of what God brings when He comes in revival is to restore the gifts, abilities and specialized knowledge or understanding that was lost when Adam and Eve fell. Adam and Eve were whole people. Sin fractured that wholeness. God comes to restore His wholeness or holiness among us. Governance was one of those things. Christians have always known God's way is the best way and a government designed that way is superior to all others. This is what the Pilgrims in America attempted to do. They read their Bibles and then set up what they understood to be a compact with what they saw in the Bible as a covenant.

Suddenly

They built God-given inalienable rights into the foundation of America's present governing system. It was meant to be a republic because such government represents the people, as opposed to a democracy, which is chaotically governed by mob rule. This is why communists, socialists, atheists, and others aligned with them, must destroy the elements within America that function as was originally intended.

The Real World Problem

They will stop at nothing to do so. No lie is too small, no endeavor too large; whether it is making sure machines have access to the Internet to change votes or to claim the nation is racist, it does not matter.[20] Their partners with specialized First Amendment rights are in the media. Their media partners have consistently lied to the people for many decades.[21] They have used their specialized rights to do so. Well, our pilgrim forebears, along with the mothers and fathers in the framing generation, gave America a group of faithful with the same rights as the media. In fact, our specialized rights precede theirs.[22] To them, this is dangerous. The faithful who can access those rights in both a physical and spiritual realm must be neutralized.

In other nations, governments easily bypass the people's rights to free speech as well as a truly free and independent press. In America,

---

[20] See Footnotes 12-13; 15-16, 21

[21] < https://ugetube.com/watch/mike-lindell-the-full-documentary-absolute-truth-election-fraud-exposed-2-5-21_OVBbgwOthuRWzb4.html > < discoverthenetworks.org > The last site is voluminous; and, it covers many decades. It is there you can read the attempt to convert America into a communistic state in many ways, including by claiming the whole country and its history is racist. Sites accessed 6/11/21.

[22] Meier, Chris, "70 Years of American Captivity: The Polity of God, The Birth of a Nation and The Betrayal of Government." 2016. Tellwell Publishers, Vancouver, British Columbia, Canada. In ebook, paperback and hardcover. Amazon link: < https://www.amazon.com/70-Years-American-Captivity-Government/dp/1773021141 >

for now, they have to make it seem as if we are still free. This is what has been going on for decades and the church has allowed it. The coup that has just taken place in America is not able to be overcome by physical means solely.[23] We will need to fight on a spiritual level as well. Let me state unequivocally from the start, that I am not espousing violence, but prayer, declaration in prayer and word and sharing the Gospel; in other words, what will affect the spiritual realm, thus seeing the effect in the natural realm.

The problem is that the church has allowed the devil to neuter us in the spiritual realm also. It is the grace of God that has allowed the whole world to see— on a working basis— what true freedom in government can look like by viewing what America's system of freedom had been. When God wraps this whole thing up with a new heaven and earth, none of that will be necessary. If Jesus tarries, then we are going to need to live in a place where communism, socialism, fascism and their religious partners cannot succeed. America was that example to the world. Now, barely Israel is the only country left. I'm still hopeful for America, but our reality and dynamic within the church must change or all will be lost.

My prayer is that this chapter can open some Christian eyes to see the truth in our Bibles that those filled with the Holy Spirit— and at the direction of the Spirit— can declare God's will for the earth and see the effect in real-world time. We must and should speak the word of God forth, judging and declaring righteousness back into our nations. Some would say our laws are not unjust.

In 2019 and 2020, the Democrat party in America at the state levels moved to pass laws to abort full-term babies; in some cases by advis-

---

[23] See Footnotes 20-21.

ing they be left to die on a table for however long that might take.[24] There are countless other unjust and ungodly laws, rules and regulations enacted by our governments worldwide.

The question becomes, what are we to do and is there Scripture for how we are to proceed? For me, personally, as I hear the word of the Lord, or get a sensing of what it is He wishes to convey, I try to get the whole of what He is sharing. By prayer and meditating upon what He is saying, I take time to learn and listen. I was taught, as a minister, we should seek the Lord's counsel before we blab what it is we feel He is saying. There are many reasons for that. One, it is an honor and responsibility to share God's word with God's people. How we minister is as important as why and what we are to minister.

Two, we are finite beings; to think we can individually share the whole of our infinite God is ludicrous, haughty and outright insane. This is the Being who flung stars into the heavens, yet created creatures so small to perform "clean-up" duty on our planet that we need microscopes to see them. Because I know how fleeting we are as humans, I feel a burden to wait before the Lord to make sure I'm sharing as complete a word as is possible for a mere human to share.

Lastly, there is a timing for a word, as well. Just because I receive an inkling of what is in the mind of the Almighty, doesn't mean I'm to blurt it out, or assume I know what's in His mind or Council concerning the timing. Also, not all messages take that long, but some do. Some messages are never shared, but remain before the Lord in

---

[24] < https://www.nationalreview.com/corner/virginia-governor-defends-letting-infants-die/ >< https://freebeacon.com/issues/northman-on-40-week-abortion-bill-infant-would-be-delivered-and-then-a-discussion-would-ensue-between-the-physicians-and-the-mother/ >< https://www.foxnews.com/opinion/virginia-is-for-infanticide-abortion-bill-leaves-me-shocked-by-whats-going-on-in-my-own-state > https://www.foxnews.com/opinion/dr-manny-alvarez-late-term-abortion-in-new-york-and-virginia-an-ob-gyns-take >< https://www.foxnews.com/politics/democratic-lawmakers-2020-candidates-mostly-silent-on-late-term-abortion-bill-backlash Sites accessed 6/19/21.

an ongoing attitude of intercession until He tells me He has answered it or the answer is on the way.

Of course, this is somewhat different from sharing prophetically in the midst of a congregation when the anointing of the Lord is present for such ministry. That is spontaneous, and it flows in a far quicker way; especially, if you are prophesying to several or more people. Nevertheless, it must be judged as true or false by the elders and the congregation, just as a pulpit or other sermon must be judged. There are, of course, protocols for doing that which this chapter is not meant to address, per se.

I'm saying this because I ask you to judge for yourselves whether or not what I will now share is supported by Scripture. Also keep in mind that there is an element here that coincides with human governmental laws. That means what we may act upon would be relevant to a country's laws. In other words, if a country allows for self defense with a gun but another country does not, a passage such as "thou shall not murder" might present different circumstances of killing that our Bibles consider as legal but a country may not.

What we must not do is judge through our emotions or judge based on human parameters. Sure, I could easily get upset over the unrighteousness I see played out around my own nation. As believers we can get angry and sin not when we are angry over this ungodliness (Ephesians 4:26-32). Yet, there is another side to the Almighty; one which wants to restore and forgive. The reality is that I'm not seeing the whole, but sharing from a glass dimly, and perfection will come when love is applied (1 Corinthians 13:12).

Remember though, our human idea of love is not always in sync with God's reality of love. The Scriptures declare unequivocally that God, Himself *IS* love (1 John 4:7). He is not some grand idea of love. He embodies and is the manifestation of what love is. God IS the definition of love. Love— believe it or not— is not based on human emotions. It is based on God's holiness in providing a sacrifice for human sin. It is why He sent His only begotten Son to die for us. While human emotion can imagine love, human emotion does not always embody this love. Let me also lay down another theologic reality:

"All scripture is given by inspiration of God, and is profitable for doctrine, for reproof, for correction, for instruction in righteousness: That the man of God may be perfect, thoroughly furnished unto all good works" (2 Timothy 3:16, 17).

We are to rightly divide the word of truth (2 Timothy 2:15). Proper exegesis and hermeneutics should be applied when sharing any pulpit message, or on any other forum where God's word is shared. I will not be deviating from those boundaries.

Our New Testament writers used the Old Testament to lay a clear foundation for what they saw as a change to the Temple system and the direction of the religious practices to come. Jesus, Himself, made it clear in many instances, but especially as recorded and written by Matthew in his gospel (Matthew 5-7), that He did not come to abolish the Law or the prophets, but to fulfill them (Matthew 5:17).

As a result, the practice for New Testament believers is to leave aside those Old Testament practices that have been updated by the New Testament. Otherwise, like any other Scripture, we may apply what can be learned by what the Old Testament reveals.

In fact, Jesus says concerning the Old Testament:

"For verily I say unto you, Till heaven and earth pass, one jot or one tittle shall in no wise pass from the law, till all be fulfilled. Whosoever therefore shall break one of these least commandments, and shall teach men so, he shall be called the least in the kingdom of heaven: but whosoever shall do and teach them, the same shall be called great in the kingdom of heaven. For I say unto you, That except your righteousness shall exceed the righteousness of the scribes and Pharisees, ye shall in no case enter into the kingdom of heaven" (Matthew 5:18-20).

Declaring Godly Judgment

What does it mean for our righteousness to "exceed" the righteousness of the former Jewish leaders? Understanding this is a key foundational principle in what I am sharing here. I am making a case for the church to assess and declare an area of judgment when believers, especially in government, commit grievous actions. I am making a case for the church to take an appropriate place where she can declare Godly judgment upon those who move in persecution. I am making a case for a place where God moves upon the church's declaration and the manifestation of God's declaration through the church is seen in the physical world. Some would say persecution goes with sharing the Gospel; NOT in America it doesn't. It also should not happen in countries where freedom-of-religion laws exist. Obviously, the Bible is clear that in the world we will experience trouble (John 16:33). I mean simply that countries with freedom of speech and religion laws cannot persecute the body of Christ legally.

First and foremost, when we accept Jesus as Lord, and agree to His sacrifice on the cross as payment for our sin, His righteousness is imputed to us (Philippians 3:9; Romans 4:1-11; 4:20-24; 5:13, 17-19; 9:30-33; 10:4; 2 Corinthians 5:21). No longer is my idea of right standing with God at work, but I take on His righteousness, based on His sacrifice for sin. This is why we can understand God's desire to forgive sinners; yet, at the same time, with the same understanding, we know God will not tolerate continual defilement, nor reside and cohabit with it. We understand there is a clear line within society of punishment for murder, rape, thievery and the like. This is not because a country is following some archaic idea of Old Testament practice.

If someone wanted to stone someone because they saw it practiced in the Old Testament, we know this to be in error because Jesus died to set sinners free. Our practice now is to share God's word of repentance and salvation, not murder folks because they don't do what we believe the Bible says they should do.

Suddenly

One of the key and overriding principles of New Testament governance is liberty and freedom in Christ. "For whom the Son sets free, is free indeed" (John 8:36). This isn't relegated to the spiritual, solely and only. The context of this passage is seen in service; in other words, what we do for and to others. John 8, starts off with the Jewish leaders bringing a women caught in adultery to Jesus. They tell him the Law— as if He didn't know it— that Moses says she should be stoned to death for her crime.

"This they said, tempting him, that they might have to accuse him. But Jesus stooped down, and with his finger wrote on the ground, as though he heard them not. So when they continued asking him, he lifted up himself, and said unto them, He that is without sin among you, let him first cast a stone at her. And again he stooped down, and wrote on the ground. And they which heard it, being convicted by their own conscience, went out one by one, beginning at the eldest, even unto the last: and Jesus was left alone, and the woman standing in the midst. When Jesus had lifted up himself, and saw none but the woman, he said unto her, Woman, where are those thine accusers? Hath no man condemned thee? She said, No man, Lord. And Jesus said unto her, Neither do I condemn thee: go, and sin no more" (John 8:6-11).

The history in America is quite different from history in other countries. American laws were developed by Christians, assuming a Christian nation. The perfect law of liberty was understood by the multitude of the founders in America as a concept in understanding that our righteousness is imputed to us by Christ. Because of this, we love our brethren in perfect love, just as Jesus loved us (John 13:34). Because of that love, we no longer desire to commit criminal acts, to harm another— force others to do as we command— but to convince them of the perfect law of liberty.

It becomes obvious that freedom of conscience is a key element of our personal governance within church doctrine. I am not condoning lawlessness, nor advocating against the death penalty. The early church understood that society had consequences for murder, rape, incest, theft, et cetera (James 1:12-16; 1 Timothy 1:9-10). Juxtapose that with the reality that we are commanded to allow our minds to be renewed (Romans 12:1-3). In this way, the perfect will of God is revealed.

We are exhorted to allow or "let this mind be in you which was also in Christ Jesus"... (Philippians 2:5-11). That word *mind* is the Greek word *phroneo*. It means mind, but it means to allow or let a certain mindset or attitude prevail. By using it, Paul was telling us that it must be our own desire and will to appropriate what is displayed by the humility of Christ. There must be a place where we can repent and be restored, even while we must pay the consequences to society for real crime, not imagined peccadillos or politically motivated persecutions.

Right standing with God, or Godly righteousness is immediately conveyed at salvation, and is like salvation in that you can't get any more saved than what you are when you accept Christ. While we are immediately sanctified, there is always the place for the Christian to be transformed into new levels of sanctification and holiness. Unlike righteousness and salvation where I can't get any more righteous or any more saved, I can be transformed in areas of my character to be more Christ-like, thus moving into different areas of wholeness and sanctification.

In so many places within the New Testament, we are told to come in agreement with God's word concerning ourselves and the atmosphere around us. This is our authority as believers. We are commanded to fast, pray, read the Bible and worship by giving of our finances, as well as our talents. There are too many New Testament passages telling us how to govern and behave in Christ that if I were to enunciate and comment on all of them, several large volumes could be written.

The American Model

America viewed one another as, not only citizens, but brothers and sisters in Christ— brother-and-sister patriots— of a new group of states, united. Church governance through Compact-covenant translated to communities which weren't governed by church doctrine, like New York, Georgia and Virginia. Even Virginia— which was a royal colony, as opposed to other colonies who developed their charters as Compact-covenant, or self-governance on steroids— eventually developed more of a Compact-covenant governance model. In fact, this form of government was considered so superior in bringing freedom "sovereignly" to citizens, that other colonies followed it.

In the beginning there was no separation between church and state. So America developed a tendency to bring Godly understanding— as seen within the pages of the Bible— into government. In fact, it is a clear understanding within America's present Compact-covenant that American government is limited. It is limited not only in economic scope but in its desire to curtail human liberties. Each aspect of the third dynamic of the compact— the Bill of Rights— is seen as a limiting authority upon government, not the other way around. Individuals are not limited in speech or religion or where they engage in healthy and proper application of, let's say gun ownership, which is a Second Amendment right. Yet, government is limited in telling Americans where and how they can practice those rights.

America continued Compact-covenant governing documents from the Declaration of Independence, through the Constitution and into the Bill of Rights. Those three form the compact, which is the same type of governance seen within early colonial church governing documents. The final type of document was seen in every colony and was developed *originally* in America by church governing documents.

This type of governing worked so well because it was coupled with a like-minded freedom and liberty type of economic policy similar to the Bible's understanding of the perfect law of liberty.[25] Capitalism espouses individual freedom and ownership in economics as opposed

---

25 Meier, Chris, "70 Years of American Captivity: The Polity of God, The Birth of a Nation and The Betrayal of Government." 2016. Tellwell Publishers, Vancouver, British Columbia, Canada. In ebook, paperback and hardcover. Amazon link: < https://www.amazon.com/70-Years-American-Captivity-Government/dp/1773021141 >

to socialism, which espouses total state control. Did ungodly people function as well? Of course, they did; but the ability to preach the Gospel was such that all knew thievery and criminality when they saw it. "But let none of you suffer as a murderer or thief or criminal or as a troublemaker" (1 Peter 4:15; NET Bible). The covenantal understanding of "do unto others as you would have them do unto you" was taken to heart and codified in American laws. This comes from Leviticus. Quite often we quote Leviticus 19:18 as, "Love your neighbor as yourself," and that is correct. But the verses before it translates from the Hebrew like this:

"You must not deal unjustly in judgment: you must neither show partiality to the poor nor honor the rich. You must judge your fellow citizen fairly. You must not go about as a slanderer among your people. You must not stand idly by when your neighbor's life is at stake. I am the Lord. You must not hate your brother in your heart. **You must surely reprove your fellow citizen so that you do not incur sin on account of him. You must not take vengeance or bear a grudge against the children of your people, but you must love your neighbor as yourself.** I am the Lord. You must keep my statutes. You must not allow two different kinds of your animals to breed, you must not sow your field with two different kinds of seed and you must not wear a garment made of two different kinds of fabric" (Leviticus 19: 15-19, NET Bible).

In other words, if you don't tell your fellow citizen when their life is at stake, you actually hate your brother. Do we really think the Lord was worried about clothes made of wool and cotton? While there was a need in the Old Testament for these laws, the New Testament makes it clear there are spiritual reasons involved. The Lord was referring to human duplicities and/or allowing duplicitous ideas to weaken righteousness. The worst of which would be in combining an adherence to Mosaic Law with a belief in Jesus Christ as Savior.

What God does not want to see is our hatreds and duplicities flowing into our Christian lives. In other words, we will keep quiet about the possible death of other citizens when they involve themselves in potentially unhealthy behavior, but we won't say anything because we don't want to offend them. Or worse, we may have a vengeance against them, so it's okay to ignore their sinful behavior and let them rot in it.

Because the immutable laws of covenant are at work in America and Israel, it is obvious from this passage when we refuse to warn about the danger of others' actions, we all suffer: "You must surely reprove your fellow citizen so that you do not incur sin on account of them." In other words, there are physical ramifications to spiritual actions. We all experience *something* in the spiritual realm when covenant is broken. If we warn our fellow citizen, then it would seem from this and other portions, we are relieved (see Ezekiel 3:17-21; 33:1-20; Luke 6:31; Matthew 7:1-5, 12; 1 Corinthians 5:1-19; Galatians 6:1-2; James 5:19).

This is why it is dangerous when the church refuses to speak up about the evils in society, or worse, condones it through behavior or complicit actions. Paul, who wrote thirteen of the twenty-seven New Testament books, did not shy away from speaking truth to power. Jesus, who clearly spoke to those in power in such a way as to make them so angry with Him that they crucified Him, was always speaking God's truth to all earthly power structures.

On an individual level, and on a church-governance level, Paul tells us that we are to remove from fellowship and turn disobedient believers over to be buffeted of satan (1 Corinthians 5:1-5). He later spoke of turning disobedient church "leaders" over to satan as well for spreading heresies (1 Timothy 1:19-20). He did this for a reason. One, perchance that the believer would repent and be saved from eternal hellfire, and two, that the church of God would remain clean and holy. Paul spoke of those "Whose end is destruction, whose God is their belly, and whose glory is in their shame, who mind earthly things" (Philippians 3:19). We are told to refuse to support those who are lazy and idle (1 Timothy 5:11-13). We are also told to expose those leaders who sin to the whole congregation (1 Timothy 5:19-20).

Americans have always considered their Christian service as functioning in two realms, the ecumenical and the civic. Early Americans viewed ministers as well as those who served their communities in governmental positions as servants. In their minds it was just like Moses and Aaron, two brothers with a one-family outreach containing two functions. They saw civic leaders, like governors, politicians, teachers and businesses as Christian brothers and sisters serving the nation or individual communities, just as if they were church leaders serving the church. It is where America gets the common understanding to "serve God and Country." They got this from the New Testament where we see the Greek word *doulos* used to mean bondservant.

It matters very little whether our brothers and sisters are serving in the church or the government. Christians serving in government are similarly responsible to adhere to the same parameters as those who function within ecumenic service only. In fact, the reason why our early countrymen experienced freedom on an individual basis is because of the removal of many archetypes of despotism and tyranny. This was directly due to how they viewed and followed their Bibles.

The lie that the American church has swallowed since Lyndon Johnson enacted the "Johnson Rule," that church leaders and the faithful are not allowed to talk about, rebuke or otherwise "get involved" in political dialog and matters affecting society is hideous. It is not in any founding documents and is not incorporated in the American Compact-covenant.

In fact, believers are supposed to speak truth to power. We are supposed to stand up to sin codified in law and practiced, especially when no actions are taken to stop it.

Suddenly

Revelation 19:7-10: "Let us be glad and rejoice, and give honor to him: for the marriage of the Lamb is come, and his wife hath made herself ready. And to her was granted that she should be arrayed in fine linen, clean and white: for the fine linen is the righteousness of saints. And he saith unto me, Write, Blessed are they which are called unto the marriage supper of the Lamb. And he saith unto me, These are the true sayings of God. And I fell at his feet to worship him. And he said unto me, See thou do it not: I am thy fellow-servant, and of thy brethren that have the testimony of Jesus: worship God: for the testimony of Jesus is the spirit of prophecy."

Chapter Twelve

When The Bride Is Compromised

When the Body of Christ is moving in faithfulness to the Holy Spirit, it's easy to hear and speak what God wishes declared to the face of the earth. But what happens when we have whole denominations refusing to turn pedophile leaders over to satan? I am not talking about staff where sin is exposed, restoration is ongoing and the sheep are still taken care of. I am not talking about proper correction of apostate leadership. That is something we must do. I am speaking about years and years of abuse by supposed members of the clergy. That isn't the only problem, though.

What happens when we have whole denominations who refuse the counsel of God and the work of half the body of Christ because they are women— and use the Bible to do so— regardless of the fact that the New Testament Greek does not condone nor support such practices? In other words, women functioned as pastors, apostles and prophets in the early church. Romans 16 names Phoebe, Mary and Pricilla. The name Junia was changed from female to male by an early manuscript scribe. She is named as one of the apostles. John wrote to "the elect lady" in his second epistle. To me there seems to be only two possibilities as to who this woman was. Either he is writing to Jesus' mother, Mary; or he is writing to a householder, who is a woman, who is the leader of the church where they meet. Either way, we are dealing with a leader in the body of Christ.

Suddenly

We have Philip's four daughters "who did prophesy" (Acts 21:9). We forget that these daughters grew up. Eusebius tells us that they became the next generation of apostles who traveled and started churches. He mentions Philip's daughters in a passage that describes a prophet by the name of Quadratus. Eusebius regards the daughters as well as Quadratus as a hallmark of prophetic ministry in the early church. He says these prophets took over from the apostles in much of their ministry to the church.

Eusebius in his own words: "AMONG those that were celebrated at that time was Quadratus, who, report says, was renowned along with the daughters of Philip for his prophetical gifts. And there were many others besides these who were known in those days, and who occupied the first place among the successors of the apostles. And they also, being illustrious disciples of such great men, built up the foundations of the churches which had been laid by the apostles in every place, and preached the Gospel more and more widely and scattered the saving seeds of the kingdom of heaven far and near throughout the whole world. For indeed most of the disciples of that time, animated by the divine word with a more ardent love for philosophy, had already fulfilled the command of the Savior, and had distributed their goods to the needy. Then starting out upon long journeys they performed the office of evangelists, being filled with the desire to preach Christ to those who had not yet heard the word of faith, and to deliver to them the divine Gospels. And when they had only laid the foundations of the faith in foreign places, they appointed others as pastors, and entrusted them with the nurture of those that had recently been brought in, while they themselves went on again to other countries and nations, with the grace and the co-operation of God. For a great many wonderful works were done through them by the power of the divine Spirit, so that at the first hearing whole multitudes of men eagerly embraced the religion of the Creator of the universe. But since it is impossible for us to enumerate the names of all that became shepherds or evangelists in the churches throughout the world in the age immediately succeeding the apostles we have recorded, as was fitting, the names of those only who have transmitted the apostolic doctrine to us in writings still extant."[26]

When we see obvious evidence of women preaching, serving and teaching in the early church, we must realize that we have misunderstood the dynamic where Paul does tell women to be silent (1 Corinthians 14:33-35). Paul gives commands in praying and prophesying to women in 1 Corinthians 11:5. This contradicts an all-encompassing edict. This is where we miss what was going on in Corinth as a city. It was on a bay, and the city across from it was Delphi. This is where the Delphic Oracle sat. She was one of three priestesses who sat over the vapors above a fissure in the chasm of the lower level of the temple. It was called the Adyton, or the inner shrine. By the way, no women were allowed in the temple, only the priestesses. They would then mumble or spout incoherent words, which would be 'translated' as speaking future fortunes from the God Apollo. These priestesses were called Pythia.

Most scholars now believe that the practices within the Corinthian church— who had to be addressed on many issues, not just this one — resembled this Delphic temple assembly far too closely for Paul's comfort. Is it any doubt that the demonic personality functioning across the bay could have easily found a home and root in the Corinthian church's practices had Paul not intervened and made the pronouncements that he did for how to function in a service? Even the commands of the plaiting of hair, as well as other symbols and examples of womanhood that he talks about come into play with the Delphic temple (1 Corinthians 7; 12:13; 11:2-16).

We cannot ignore how the very action of hearing God and speaking to the body of Christ what we hear (1 Corinthians 12-14) would have been in jeopardy if the Corinthian church would have assimilated some of what they saw in Delphi. Generations of Christian assem-

---

[26] Eusebius, Church History, 3.37. Translated by Rev. Arthur Cushman McGiffert, edited by Drs. Philip Schaff and Henry Wace, NY, NY, 1890. Digital version published by Christian Life School of Theology, Columbus, GA, pp. 248 & 249.

blies could have missed Godly revelation had the Holy Spirit not inspired Paul to write what he did to them.

I want to be clear when I write about women in the body of Christ that I am not speaking about proper submission within family units. We will discuss this dynamic in a later chapter. It's obvious that within a household and within the intimacy of a Christian marriage, order must be maintained (Ephesians 5:21-6:4). We've got to be real with ourselves, though.

Let's ask this question: does the woman written about in Proverbs 31 seem like a child? Why are we espousing child-like behavior to wives and mothers in some Christian households? Why are we neutralizing the army of the Lord in battle?

This period of time of revival will have dynamics associated with revelation of our futures in heaven as well as immediate plans God has. There is a reason God has given human beings as gifts, or bondslaves (doulos) to the body of Christ (Ephesians 4:11-16). It's so the body joins together in love, defying the world's systems and implementing Christ's narrative and way of doing things as our constant. Early America did that in her infancy, and the world watched our freedoms promote a wealthy society. Many of them wanted to come here, and they did. This is how we are to function inside the church by creating heaven on earth. We then see God's promises reveal His wholeness and we facilitate and extend that to everyone.

It should not be located in one region, but must extend to cover the whole planet. This means that we must also see Godly discipline as well as order. That's the only way we can realize what revival is sent to accomplish. That's why signs and wonders are seen. That's why all of God's servants and vessels need to function, from the littlest child to the elder statesman. It also means we don't allow every crazy worldly idea to creep among the Body. What has crept into the local church today?

When The Bride Is Compromised

Corruption

Are we immune to the new requirements in New York, Virginia and other parts of the world concerning infanticide and abortion creeping into the church? Are we developing a cynical and demonic cheapening-of-life attitude? We vote for, and refuse to call out government leaders who readily light public buildings emblazoning their demonic celebrations.[27]

Who is next in line for death after unwanted or deformed infants? Will it be Christians, Jews or grandma? What are we to do when Sunday is actually the most segregated day in many nations? Why are we so squeamish in talking about these practices of European socialism with infanticide, euthanasia, and its obvious control over the Democrat Party in America as well as other governments of the world? Why won't we talk about the racism of socialism and its mirror image to satan's seduction of mankind in the Garden of Eden?[28]

Why do we talk about or prosecute corruption when one political party allegedly commits it, but ignore it when a different party com-

---

[27] < https://www.foxnews.com/opinion/virginia-is-for-infanticide-abortion-bill-leaves-me-shocked-by-whats-going-on-in-my-own-state> <https://www.foxnews.com/faith-values/ob-gyn-rejects-ny-abortion-law-absolutely-no-reason-to-kill-a-baby-in-third-trimester>< https://wchstv.com/news/offbeat/baphomet-statue-one-step-closer-to-being-on-state-capitol-grounds > This next link is an article arguing Christian support for this demon sitting in Oklahoma. I do not support that, but I place it here to show how convoluted we become. < https://sojo.net/articles/why-christians-should-support-satanic-statue-oklahoma >< https://www.youtube.com/watch?v=sluZOzgkwrc >< https://www.lawenforcementtoday.com/bidens-secretary-of-state-orders-lgbt-flags-flown-at-u-s-embassies/ >

[28] https://www.ccm4worldwideworship.org/page-2.html See both subtitles: "Economics & the Bible" and "The Lie".

mits even worse crimes, and practices witchcraft openly?[29] Why do whole denominations neglect telling their flocks about fasting, baptisms, healings, signs and wonders? Why are we so hesitant to talk about speaking truth to power?

Is it because we are afraid; is it the fear of money and man? Is it because of our own denomination's malfeasance in those areas? Is it because we don't know? Is it because we don't understand the ramifications? Is it because we think there are no consequences to our sin? Do Hosea, Zephaniah and Zechariah have something to tell us about ourselves and the nations we live in? Are there any similarities in this history we can learn from? Let's take a look and see.

Hosea, Zephaniah and Zechariah

We have to understand a little Jewish history in order to see a more complete picture as it relates to modern countries, including America. A world power in her day, Babylon kept vassal states in and around the Asian continent. Egypt was its own power and none too happy when she saw many around her coming under Assyria and Babylon's influence. This is why you see referenced warnings among the Old Testament prophets not to rely on Egypt to protect them, but to rely on their God (Isaiah 30:3). Instead, many Jews developed a penchant for sacrificing to, and seeking answers from, idols belonging to various warring lands over the course of her history (Micah 1:5-7). Some of those idols required sacrificing children to them, not just wine and animals (2 Kings 16:3; 17:31; 23:10; Jeremiah 7:30-32; 19:3-5).

Israel was split as a country in those days between Israel proper— or the northern country— and Judah, who had specific oversight of the Temple and Jerusalem. Israel becomes a "client" state, or what we

---

[29] https://www.infowars.com/spirit-cooking-clinton-campaign-chairman-invited-to-bizarre-satanic-performance/ There is no proof that anyone but celebrities and other democrats attended this woman's "services." Nevertheless, the email-invitation was sent to Clinton campaign boss, Podesta. There seems to be no evidence he attended. (There is no hyphen in the url between the word invited.)

would view as a vassal of Assyria. Israel pays tribute to her and sought protection, or common ground in battle, if another country came to pick a fight. Judah refuses allegiances which compromise her sovereignty, but not Israel. God, Israel's husband, is not pleased with this. He did not make his people to become pawns in other nation's fights, nor to be looted by them in national agreements.

He sends Hosea to start preaching His displeasure with their national "arrangements" by telling Hosea to take a harlot and raise children of harlotry. He did this to let them know how he felt when they offer idols worship and make allegiances with foreign nations which impact their sovereignty. Is He doing this to be mean? Is He doing this because He doesn't want them to 'have friends'? Or to be a meaningful part of the global community? Or is it because He raised them up as a free nation and where they go in captivity, He goes in captivity? We know God Almighty will not be taken captive, so Israel will be left destitute and on her own.

Hosea preaches primarily to Israel in the northern country, from 785 BCE. He starts some 180 years before a battle in 605 BCE takes place. That battle, known as the battle of Carchemish is when Judah starts paying tribute to Babylon. It is long before that battle that Hosea warns Israel not to become cozy with the Assyrians. This is because Babylon will come on the scene and overtake what the Assyrians had formerly controlled. Little Israel, instead of listening to the prophets— to God Almighty— will become a pawn, a pinball in a grasp for power and territory.

As we can see from the Bible, Israel doesn't listen and is taken into captivity. Before Israel in the North is taken captive, Judah is mixed in her opinion. Some in Judah say they should side with Egypt and seek protection there, others say no.

King Josiah spearheads the temple revival in Judaea, but is killed in battle in 609 BCE in Megiddo with the Egyptians. These battles set up the defeat of Pharaoh Necho's army in 605 BCE, which precipitates the beginning of three different time periods of captivity for Judah.[30]

There are many years dividing Hosea's preaching and final captivity for the whole nation. The son of Beeri, a contemporary of Isaiah and Micah, he prophesied to Israel during the reigns of Uzziah, Jotham, Ahaz, Hezekiah and Jeroboam, the son of Jehoash of Israel. God gave them plenty of time to repent and change their national ways, but they did not. God sends a few of the prophets in a concurrent fashion at various different times in this history. He usually sends more than one. Our Old Testament is full of what Christianity has called major and minor prophets. All sent with one goal in mind: to spare God's people from the consequences of their sin, if they will but listen.

One of those prophets, sent to Judah in around 630 BCE, is Zephaniah. He is a direct descendant of King Hezekiah, prophesying during King Josiah's reign, probably before the temple revivals. He calls for repentance and, barring that, the eventual and future glory of Israel once they realize their mistake (2 Kings 22-23; Zephaniah 1:1; 2:1-3; 3:14-20). The revival must have seemed like a fulfillment for those who remember his preaching. It is, but it is not the totality. Remember, Josiah will be killed in battle within 25 years and Judah will begin her captivity.

Another prophet named Zechariah comes on the scene around 520 BCE, some hundred years later. Israel has already failed, been taken captive and has come back to the land to rebuild. He is the son of Berekiah (1:1) and is a contemporary of Haggai, both writing some of the Psalms together. He joins with him in prophesying repentance to the Jews when the Temple was being rebuilt. He is honored with penning several important Messianic Scriptures (Zechariah 9:9-10; 12:10; 13:7). Yet, there is still more history to come. A wall must be

---

[30] Remember when dealing with BC or BCE history that the numbers count down instead of up when recording events. So Josiah will be killed in 609, and then the 605 battle will begin time periods for Judah's captivity.

built and Nehemiah will be sent by King Artaxerxes to accomplish this task. This is because the Jews who had been sent back with the first two expeditions would become distracted by those around them, and complacent in their own lives.

There had been three groups of Jews sent back from the captivity to rebuild Jerusalem.[31] Nehemiah is among the last, warning them that their own sovereignty as a people will be in question if they do not act to remove what is distracting them and complete the building of the wall around the city.

Connecting the Dots

What parallels for modern America can be drawn? Are there similar patterns with other nations for global revival? We have to remember that God does not see time as we do. Hundreds of years passed from Hosea to Zechariah, the destruction and the rebuilding of the Temple and the wall. What sent Israel into captivity was, first and foremost the neglect to follow the Lord's commands. Have we done so in America, as a church? Yes, we have. We have neglected to teach our Compact-covenant design of government to our children, as well. The body of Christ worldwide has the same problem. There is a neglect in following the Lord's commands, as well as not teaching our children the tremendous benefit biblical Christianity has in keeping us aware and able to govern ourselves.

In fact, the problem is so acute that today we have people who actually believe that the foreign ideology known as socialism is more

---

[31] See my article from April 2017, where I compare Nehemiah's building efforts to what I saw as emblematic of America's possible future < https://nebula.wsimg.com/1e02c8b312ba62130d4104e69a0977b5?AccessKeyId=D1B765CBBC658EF49FE8&disposition=0&alloworigin=1 > For a broad history surrounding the Babylonian captivity see < https://en.wikipedia.org/wiki/Babylonian_captivity > While Wikipedia is known for errors, in this article, the exact dates are not as important for me as the events and behind the scenes attitudes of the participants. Wikipedia gives us that in a concise way with one click.

Suddenly

compassionate, prosperous and "just" than America's original economic and governing design. This is not just factually incorrect, the science was proven by Ludvig von Mises in, around, and after 1920.[32] Many the world over will complain that without socialism we cannot take care of marginalized people. Creating a safety net is not truly helpful with socialism.[33] First, the church, the body of Christ is to be that safety net. When we will not or cannot do so, many nations develop systems whereby they pay into the safety net; this is not socialism.

In America, I would argue that we would be better off in free market stocks than Social Security or Medicare, but neither program is socialistic. In the footnotes you will see proof that socialism and communism are satanic to the core. I'm not saying capitalism is pure. It is what you choose it to be. That is not the case concerning socialism or communism. There are pastors and churches who espouse both ideologies and vote that way in America. That means we are in open rebellion to Godly counsel. These ideologies are not American, but were started on foreign soil.

Why is it that billions come to America to escape their own country's socialistic-communistic economic policies? Is it because capitalism and Compact-covenant republican government must somehow be mean, inept and unproductive? That's what socialists will try to tell you. In 2013, Venezuela developed socialistic policies that took

---

[32] < https://www.econlib.org/library/Columns/y2018/HorwitzSocialism.html >
< https://oll.libertyfund.org/titles/mises-selected-writings-of-ludwig-von-mises-vol-1-monetary-and-economic-problems-before-during-and-after-the-great-war >

[33] < https://www.ccm4worldwideworship.org/page-2.html > This is page two, scroll down to the titles "Economics and the Bible" and "The Lie" to read a concise reason why socialism cannot succeed from both natural science as well as the biblical record.

her citizens' guns and by 2017, Venezuelans were eating their dogs.34 Freedom in liberty always goes hand in hand with economic freedom. By the way, Europe is bankrupt and the Danish countries socialists tout are not funded by socialism but by capitalism.35

Israel allowed other nations to dictate her worship, attitude and laws. This led to her economic downfall. First, she worshipped their idols, then she dressed and acted like they did. Finally, they captured her resources and stole her economy. There are always steps to this encroachment. Barriers keep many problems out. But barriers/walls alone can't help a people who worship idols. Socialism weaves and sends miscues all in an effort to hide its true intentions. It really is an idol attempting to govern who and what you are. It wants anything and everything you own. God exposes all intentions and, if you will look at the multitude of footnotes, the science proves the true intentions of socialism. When we, as His people, refuse His counsel, we are doomed to repeat the history of failure.

Is There Not a Cause?

We do have a lifeline. It is the Bible, God's word; it is the Holy Spirit, the precious third member of the Trinity who was sent to lead and

---

34 < https://www.foxnews.com/world/venezuelans-regret-gun-prohibition-we-could-have-defended-ourselves >< https://www.usatoday.com/story/news/world/2016/05/18/venezuela-food-shortages-cause-some-hunt-dogs-cats-pigeons/84547888/ >

35 < https://www.express.co.uk/finance/city/662052/Britain-set-for-BANKRUPTCY-amid-1-85-TRILLION-of-HIDDEN-debt >< https://www.independent.co.uk/life-style/health-and-families/health-news/nhs-uk-now-has-one-of-the-worst-healthcare-systems-in-the-developed-world-according-to-oecd-report-a6721401.html > <https://www.telegraph.co.uk/news/0/european-debt-crisis-not-just-greece-drowning-debt/ > <https://www.foxnews.com/politics/americans-warming-to-socialism-over-capitalism-polls-show > <https://www.thelocal.dk/20151101/danish-pm-in-us-denmark-is-not-socialist > < https://papers.ssrn.com/sol3/papers.cfm?abstract_id=514242 > The last link only records privatization to 2004, the previous statements by the president of Denmark to Sanders would indicate they have become more capitalistic.

guide us into all truth. In America, our national covenant is between believing and non-believing peoples. We, as God's people have the responsibility to cry out to Him when our covenant partners are placing us in jeopardy. Let me refer you to 1 Peter 4:17: *"For the time is come that judgment must begin at the house of God: and if it first begin at us, what shall the end be of them that obey not the gospel of God?"*

The understanding in the Greek is threefold. One, if God's judgment begins with God's people, and they are barely saved, what will become of the sinner? Two, "at the house of God," can be translated "from the house of God." In other words, we must see the church or saint judged first and since we are not seeing that now, then it is not time for the unbelieving to be judged.

There is a third sense here from the context of the epistle. It is clear Peter is talking to a group of Christians who are not being attacked for doing ungodly or criminal behavior, but for following God. They are being attacked by unbelievers. This attack is in violation of the brotherhood of mankind seen from Genesis (Cain and Abel) and its covenant, mankind to mankind.

So the church, as the plaintiff in petitioning God, can begin to speak with the word of God and command realignment (hence judgment beginning from the house of God). I believe all three aspects of translation are seen here, especially in light of other passages in the New Testament of the church being light and salt and a hindering force to satan (Matthew 5:14; Matthew 5:13; 2 Thessalonians 2:3-8). In secular or non-sectarian terms, the covenant of mankind to mankind can be religious. Even when it is not, we can still function with covenantal attitude.

Concerning those who claim Christianity but still vote socialist-communist, or parties who support such ideologies, they are refusing Godly counsel exposing the dangers surrounding these forms of governance. They must be brought before the Lord and turned over to the enemy, perchance their own souls might be saved and they may repent. You cannot claim Christianity while you support and condone infanticide.[36] You cannot claim Christianity while you condone immorality. Of course, their respective church leaders are directed to do this by Paul.

For those of you who say this was for sexual immorality only, let me ask you a question. Why do you think so many abort babies in many countries around the world? Is it because as husbands and wives they decide killing their children is easier? Or is it because we have rampant groups of people— many claiming to be Christian— having sex outside the marital covenant?

I am not saying there cannot be exceptions to rules. In a case where the mother's life is at stake is an exception. The situations where rape and abuse happen and a child is conceived can also be seen as exceptions to some rules. Obviously, no one should demand a woman give birth to her rapist or abuser's child— even though this is not the innocent child's fault— adoption is a better outcome. But, as in the case when a mother's life is at stake, these must be private decisions made between her and her support system. The only responsibility a governing body has, is to capture the offender so he can't do this to someone else's daughter.

Let's be very clear that this biblical response should be for those claiming Christianity. People have free will. Each one of us must stand before God one day. But if we as leaders don't let the flock of God know that we must hold them to a higher standard than the world does, when will they learn that? We must exhort them in the reading of the word or the washing of the word and the Spirit. We must be discipling the body of Christ. We should be sharing the grace of God that helps all of us to live holy lives because the Spirit of God is leading us by His righteousness and keeps us in right relationship to Him.

---

[36] https://www.foxnews.com/opinion/dr-manny-alvarez-late-term-abortion-in-new-york-and-virginia-an-ob-gyns-take

Suddenly

Some would disagree at my calling for the same treatment for political leaders who espouse socialism and abortion on demand, and all manner of immoral practices. In America, when they claim Christianity and run for political office, they are under the same relationship to Christ as any other believer. I would argue that's true in other countries.

Even if they do not claim Christ and they target God's people, we have a remedy with the Compact-covenant for God to intervene. In other countries, biblical norms would apply solely. What I mean by that is all Christians are directed by the Bible to lead many to the Lord and disciple them in the ways of Christ. If and when Christian government leaders continually refuse this counsel as politicians, their very souls and the souls of nations are at stake. We have no other recourse as elders in the body of Christ except to turn them over to the enemy; perchance, they may be saved and repent, thus bringing nations back from the precipice of annihilation.

Suddenly

Proverbs 1:7; 20-22: "*The fear of the LORD is the beginning of knowledge: but fools despise wisdom and instruction.*" "*Wisdom crieth without; she uttereth her voice in the streets: She crieth in the chief place of concourse, in the openings of the gates: in the city she uttereth her words, saying, How long, ye simple ones, will ye love simplicity? And the scorners delight in their scorning, and fools hate knowledge?*"

Psalm 2:8: "*Ask of me, and I shall give thee the heathen for thine inheritance, and the uttermost parts of the earth for thy possession.*"

Matthew 7:7-8: "*Ask, and it shall be given you; seek, and ye shall find; knock, and it shall be opened unto you: For every one that asketh receiveth; and he that seeketh findeth; and to him that knocketh it shall be opened.*"

Chapter Thirteen

Revival To The Nations

It always looks to us as if God works backwards, when in reality it is us who hold chaos in our members. God restores and redeems what is lost and broken. I've mentioned a few things that were both lost and became broken as a result of the fall of man. So from the foundation of planet Earth, God sowed Christ as an offering to redeem mankind (1 Peter 1:19-20; Ephesians 1:4-5). Broken man founded broken nations. Each nation has a God-given call and destiny to restore and/or help something broken on the planet. Israel's unique call was to show forth covenant as governance and to gift Messiah to mankind. She was chosen by God to do this.

America was birthed to display all the riches that following the God of covenant brings to a nation of heathen when they obey that same God. Each nation has a call and a destiny and none of it can be realized when they have no wisdom in this area of biblical understanding. So God sends the people who can birth revivals of wisdom and understanding.

These, in turn, give rise to nations with the same revelation. It is the devil's desire to get nations to spout his narrative and come in agreement with him instead of the word of God. This is the real reason why a virus was used to lock people down. A virus that kills less than two percent of the population would never be able to be used that way unless there was a plan. When you lock down people, you

Suddenly

lock down Christians who can proclaim the word of God, thus attempting to lock down God's deliverance for nations.

In the Bible, it is the foolish nation that is likened to harlots. Let me be clear that it is a simile. I'm highlighting a figure of speech to make a point. Thankfully, Jesus is in the harlot-redeeming business. Let me also be clear that harlotry is not limited to women only. I've seen my fair share of men trying to play the harlot. We are all sinners until God finds us and redeems us. He can do that for nations as well. But in the Bible's understanding, it is the harlot that goes about trapping the foolish.

I'm going to juxtapose that to the nonsense that was spilled over the airwaves about viruses. When there are five or more better drugs that can cure a virus, and then God-given human immune systems which scavenge all variations of said virus better than any vaccine that purports to change human immune systems— thus making them weaker to all variants— someone is playing someone as a fool.[37]

I believe God is coming in revival to restore the destiny of all nations that will receive Him. To that end as Christians, we must speak truth to power and speak the word of God in declaratory fashion as He declares it be done. I don't want to belabor a point here, but if politicians do not claim Christianity and make no attack against the

---

[37]This video contains discussions between many specialists: military doctors, immunologists, etc. I believe only one is Christian, the rest are of various new-age religions. I mention that because they each get a chance at the end of the video to express their religious opinions. Their hearts are to get this information out to the public, having been silenced so many times by the media. Grab this while you can; I'm not sure how long before it is scrubbed. < https://www.bitchute.com/video/EzhjSE0H5VHE > This next video is from various doctors as well, also discussing the vaccine's frightening side-effects; the worst being death of over 13,000 people. For that number they use the American vaers.hhs.gov reporting agency. The same problems exist from Big Tech; prayerfully, it will still be available by the time you view it. < https://forbidden-knowledgetv.net/doctors-around-the-world-issue-dire-warning-do-not-get-the-covid-vaccine/ > More updated and stable URL: <covid.daystar.com

bride of Christ, then sharing the Gospel is our best method in helping our respective nations.

In the United States, many politicians claim both leadership and Christianity as a result of the unique American governing compact understanding. That means they are subject as any leader in the church would be subject to correction. For those who claim Christianity but are not politicians, then their individual church leaders must convince them of unrighteousness. If they refuse Godly counsel, they must be turned over by their respective church leaders to our enemy, perchance their souls may be saved. Our only hope for the unbelieving politician, is for us to cry out to the Lord in prayer that they are in violation of our various country's governmental agreements.

In America, the church can do as the signers to the Declaration of Independence did. By the way, that is compacted with our Constitution and Bill of Rights. They can petition the "Supreme Judge of the world," and "with a reliance on the Protection of Divine Providence,"[38] they can ask Him to come into this disagreement and bring them back in line with freedom, liberty and justice for all.

Why do I encourage this type of action? Am I being vindictive or promoting some kind of control and manipulative interpretation of the Scriptures? Have I forgotten the grace, love and kindness of the Lord in leading us to repentance? We must remember the goal here is not pain and suffering, but repentance so souls may be saved, and for the cleansing of our land and/or the house of God. I am encouraging spiritual action, not physical retribution. First, spiritual action must be reserved for specific congregations by their leaders in spiritual leadership over them.

---

[38] Our Library of Congress has a site in which you can click on either the Declaration in the Journals of the Continental Congress of 1776, or a Broadside. That site is < https://www.loc.gov./rr/program/bib/ourdocs/DeclarInd.html > One site for many of our federal documents < http://avalon.law.yale.edu/subject_menus/18th.asp > for the Declaration in particular < http://avalon.law.yale.edu/18th_century/declare.asp >

Suddenly

In America, believing citizens within that compact may petition heaven to bring their unbelieving counterparts back in line with the compact. That's because of the non-denominational, Compact-covenant that is in effect in that country. They may, as I see it, also reserve spiritual authority to those rulers who claim Christianity, but refuse all Godly counsel in government to be buffeted by the enemy, perchance they may repent and be truly saved. Whatever nation we reside in, we must take authority as the Scriptures encourage us to do.

I realize some would say, "Well, if they want abortion and other things you don't agree with, who are you to try and stop that? Even a covenant between individuals can be changed." In that I would agree. However, there isn't a country on the planet who could claim any sense of moral judgment to codify murder of innocent children. This is not some mere disagreement over abortion or the right of free individuals to make changes to governing documents when all involved agree with the change. This is the outright support for, and shelter to, murderers and those who wish to justify infanticide. There was no medical reason for the changes that were seen within the United States' legal system.[39]

Defilement

In fact, when any nation decides to change a law from righteousness in order to support deadly practices, all of us have a responsibility to stop it. Even though Americans have a different national understanding in law than other nations do, there are dangers here for all in many nations. It is clear Hosea, Zephaniah and Zechariah were written to the nation of Israel concerning her ability to dwell in her land; yet, it seems clear from the rest of Jesus' teaching in Matthew, that

---

[39] < https://www.foxnews.com/opinion/dr-kent-ingle-pro-abortion-bills-across-country-are-inhumane-repugnant-and-vile > < https://www.foxnews.com/opinion/dr-manny-alvarez-late-term-abortion-in-new-york-and-virginia-an-ob-gyns-take > < https://www.foxnews.com/opinion/new-yorks-democrats-think-that-a-fully-formed-unborn-child-is-less-important-than-the-average-house-cat >

God does not change. In other words, like Israel, blessing could extend to all those who are God's children when they form a covenant government, asking God into it; or conversely, cursing may take place when they disobey that covenant.

We must understand God does not desire to harm us. We are doing this to ourselves by our repeated sin. Repeated sin produces spiritual as well as physical results to our land and atmosphere. Where's my proof, you say? We have instances where the Bible tells us that the land will spit us out (Leviticus 18:25-28). Or, more particularly, there is a defilement which can be brought to any land where there is a breakdown in morality.

This breakdown is first seen in the home; hence the laws seen within the Scriptures encouraging the unity of the home in expressing the teaching of Yahveh (Deuteronomy 4:26, 33, 40; 32:46-47). While Israel's captivity was because she disobeyed God, in its infancy, this disobedience was precipitated by a breakdown in the home (Ezekiel 22:7, 15). This is why we see a promise in Malachi where 'Elijah' would come at the end of the age. He comes to turn the hearts of the children and the parents— the word fathers is specifically used in Malachi— toward each other again (Malachi 4:1-6). So it would seem this principle must also be seen in the New Testament, and it is.

As is the case with the rest of the Decalogue, this law is applicable to us, but Jesus goes further. In Matthew 5, Jesus refers to laws concerning neighbors. He does the same with the commandment concerning honoring parents: "That ye maybe the children of your Father which is in heaven . . . Be ye therefore perfect, even as your Father which is in heaven is perfect" (Matthew 5:45). So there is a principle that if we do not honor our parents, for whatever reason, and do not repent of it, as well as ask the Holy Spirit to root out those thought patterns which continue that dishonoring, it can affect our relationship to God.

I can't think of anything more dishonoring of our parents than the intentional law within ObamaCare in the United States, when it

Suddenly

formed IPAB boards to see which elderly among the sick was least deserving of medical care. That doesn't even include the theft of $700 billion from the elderly Medicare program to form Obama-Care.[40] Of course, American politicians have "borrowed" money from their elders' Social Security plan for decades. So much so, that it will be insolvent by 2034.[41] Add to this hypocrisy the killing of children in the womb up until nine-month's gestation, and we have American land that has been defiled.

So America is an example to the world of how awesome it is for a country to follow Godly governmental practices, and how awful it is when we run away from those practices. Add all of the similar immorality up in other lands, and it can be seen as a defilement over the land of the whole planet. In other words, an encouragement for human as well as demonic strongholds to pollute the place we occupy here, as well as the place in our soul where rest and peace could be seen if we would follow the counsel of God.

We've all heard more and more socialists touting the need to curb global warming's effects by instituting more laws. More laws will not help a world filled with rebellious nations murdering, killing, and stealing in order to foster voter fraud and theft through taxation. These are soul-based spiritual defilements. God's laws are simple; when you defile your fellow neighbor, you defile your land. God Almighty put covenant in place from the beginning of the planet.

---

[40] < https://www.washingtontimes.com/news/2017/jun/14/obamacare-death-panels-should-be-ended/ > < https://www.healthinsurance.org/faqs/what-is-this-controversy-regarding-the-ipab-really-about/ > < https://www.washingtonpost.com/news/wonk/wp/2012/08/14/romneys-right-obamacare-cuts-medicare-by-716-billion-heres-how/?noredirect=on&utm_term=.326f7df34365 > < https://www.amazon.com/Inside-National-Health-California-Milbank/dp/0520270193 >

[41] <https://www.forbes.com/sites/merrillmatthews/2011/07/13/what-happened-to-the-2-6-trillion-social-security-trust-fund/#1d394a494947><https://www.usatoday.com/story/money/personalfinance/retirement/2018/11/18/social-security-how-much-congress-owes-interest-over-next-decade/38532839/

With the kind of immorality taking place, it seems we have defilement going on all over the planet.

Ask for the Nations and Speak Truth to Power

This is why we must see revival over every nation on the globe. You would be right if you are reading this thinking I am warning many nations that their captivity can be realized by foreign enemy forces. It's not just in the future; many nations have already been infiltrated.

Socialism, communism, various religious enterprises condoning abortion, infanticide, euthanasia and giving the hard-earned finances of citizens over to legal and illegal immigrants is holding billions captive. These ideologies incentivize citizens' money being handed over to a new voting block because many citizens won't do what these immoral politicians want anymore.[42]

Satellites in geosynchronous orbit from various countries are in danger from China. They are the most sensitive satellites that we possess. They tell us missile launch moment. They are now threatening orbital regimes like America. At the start of any war, all China would have to do would be to knock out these satellites. We would be unable to defend ourselves. Hey, with Hollywood's help they could make it look like aliens were invading us. It would throw us back to World War 2 capabilities.

In 2007, China took out one of their own satellites. In May 2013, they sent a missile to take out a satellite in 30,000 kilometer space. Russia already launched a satellite that can cozy up to another satellite to take it out. In 2006, President Bush wanted to develop such a satellite but the Democrat Party congress refused to give him the money. Former President Obama has refused to give any weight to develop such weapons.[43] We have a weapons race in space that no-

---

[42] < https://sdgs.un.org/2030agenda >

[43] https://www.warhistoryonline.com/war-articles/china-conducts-secret-hypersonic-missile-launch-amid-growing-concerns-over-its-nuclear-capabilities.html

body but President Trump addressed. Now you know why voting machines were compromised in 2020.

These behaviors encourage poverty among all nation's citizens. This allows for a cheapening of all societies by weakening laws surrounding the sanctity of life as well as hard, ethical work. Eventually, humans no longer place a premium on life. Instead, they place a premium on their own needs. It's no longer what can you do for your country, but what can you steal from others?

Socialism isn't about making things more equitable. This is how they draw you in. They lie that you can own anything in common, therefore, you can share in common funds. The science proves you cannot.[44] But remember, this is the hook. All this "giving"— it really is corruptive stealing— comes at a price. The price is not just an individual's economic freedom, it is the civic and civil liberties and freedoms all individuals in a nation experience as a result of their country's specific governing documents.

In America, those were exact and far reaching. This is why the devil had to take as long as he did to hold America captive. It started in the 1900s with Teddy Roosevelt and Woodrow Wilson. California, New York, Michigan, to name a few American states, have enacted quite a few policies encouraging socialism. Is it possible for California to fall off into the ocean and away from America? I would hate to see that happen but geology shifts, and I would never ignore the spiritual ramifications as an early precursor to the captivity of America. We never make the connection between our spiritual filth and the upheaval we see environmentally, ecologically and where we live.

This is all part and parcel to Jesus' words about the land spitting us out. Do you know typhus, the disease seen in medieval earth is having a roaring revival in Los Angeles? California is not as solvent as she

---

[44] < https://www.ccm4worldwideworship.org/page-2.html > This is page two, scroll down to the titles "Economics and the Bible" and "The Lie" to read a concise reason why socialism cannot succeed from both natural science as well as the biblical record.

seems. Socialistic policies make owning a home impossible in many areas of the state. She spends the money necessary to help the homeless on illegals, and the homeless defecate in the streets; garbage piles up and storm drains carry the filth abroad. This attracts rats as they populate the street camps where the homeless live, spreading the flea infestation to city hall itself.[45] This is one instance of how attitude translates to policy and policy translates to misery.

Of course, America is not the only country where communistic-type policies defile the Earth's land. John Adams, the second president of the United States, made a similar observation when he wrote an October 11, 1798, letter to the officers of the First Brigade of the Third Division of the Militia of Massachusetts:

"While our country remains untainted with the principles and manners which are now producing desolation in so many parts of the world; while she continues sincere, and incapable of insidious and impious policy, we shall have the strongest reason to rejoice in the local destination assigned us by Providence. But should the people of America once become capable of that deep simulation towards one another, and towards foreign nations, which assumes the language of justice and moderation while it is practicing iniquity and extravagance, and displays in the most captivating manner the charming pictures of candor, frankness, and sincerity, while it is rioting in rapine and insolence, this country will be the most miserable habitation in the world; because we have no government armed with power capable of contending with human passions unbridled by morality and religion. Avarice, ambition, revenge, or gallantry, would break the strongest cords of our Constitution as a whale goes through a net. Our Constitution was made only for a moral and religious people. It is wholly inadequate to the government of any other."[46]

---

[45] < http://www.foxla.com/news/local-news/city-worker-infected-in-la-typhus-outbreak > < https://video.foxnews.com/v/5998442627001/#sp=show-clips >

[46] Charles Francis Adams, "The Works of John Adams, Second President of the United States: with a Life of the Author, Notes, and Illustration." Boston, 1854: Little, Brown and Co. Volume 9. 228, 229. In the public domain.

Suddenly

Time has not changed this dynamic. All countries of the planet experience demonic foothold situations as soon as they depart from Godly government. This is why we must see all nations revived. God comes to revive nations in order to kick out the intruding spiritual forces holding them captive. The Bible does tell us that in the last days the devil will do so many various signs and wonders that even the very elect can be fooled by them. Satan doesn't do this because he is so successful. He does this because he is desperate.

When God moves in reviving nations and the church becomes serious in asking for nations, the devil goes over the top to try to stop this. We must recognize when we've become the lobster in the cooking pot. While in cold water, the danger isn't as obvious. Over time as generations are born outside of the freedoms of God-given human rights, they forget how free they were: no regulations and a whole lot less taxes.

Of course, this pales in comparison to communistic countries who control where you live, how you eat, what you wear and what you do with your life and the lives of your children. In those countries you own nothing; the inhuman entity called the state owns all. This is the devil's sliding park. You start at the top in God's kingdom, and before you know it, you've slidden into hell for all eternity. God exhorts us to ask for the nations. He wants to stop the devil's slide-and-fun park. The devil's park is all smoke and mirrors; it's Hollywood on steroids until you die. You can't believe what you are looking at because all or most of it is a fake.

You think I'm crazy? Have you gone to a movie lately? It all looks so real. If you've been successful in viewing the footnotes and the discussions among doctors on some of the websites, you know these vaccines do not protect anyone against a virus. All they can do is make the virus less about killing you. But, as you have seen as well in the footnotes, there are cheap and safe drugs that can cure you. How often did you hear about them? It all looked so real, didn't it?

They fooled the world and for very good reasons: they got rid of a president who was a thorn in their sides; they shut down the churches and other voices which contradict their narrative; and lastly, they consolidated power. It was a power grab from the start. They got rid of a man that wanted to stop one nation from controlling the world. The devil needs mankind to be under one system of government the world over. When that happens, he can control the world easily. Many different countries with God's word being spoken into the atmosphere are not easily dissuaded. An ideology like communism-socialism makes controlling the world a lot easier. It's only the precursor to trouble.

Before we close out this chapter I'd like to share something from John's Gospel the Lord highlighted to me. All across the world, this is what revival will be about: "Then spake Jesus again unto them, saying, I am the light of the world: he that followeth me shall not walk in darkness, but shall have the light of life" (John 8:12). Light dispels darkness and revival of Godly light brings Godly life. I am convinced revival can go on all over the world, even while the world is experiencing great trouble. We must make the decision not to look at the trouble, but to God (Psalm 46:1).

Jesus said something else: "All that ever came before me are thieves and robbers: but the sheep did not hear them. I am the door: by me if any man enter in, he shall be saved, and shall go in and out, and find pasture. The thief cometh not, but for to steal, and to kill, and to destroy: I am come that they might have *life, and that they might have it more **abundantly**.* I am the good shepherd: the good shepherd giveth his life for the sheep. But he that is an hireling, and not the shepherd, whose own the sheep are not, seeth the wolf coming, and leave the sheep, and flee: and the wolf catch them, and scatter the sheep. The hireling flees, because he is an hireling, and care not for the sheep. I am the good shepherd, and know my sheep, and am known of mine" (John 10:8-14).

Jesus told everyone that He is the good shepherd, laying His life down for the sheep. He also said that the hireling cuts and runs.

Suddenly

While we are watching Jesus move in signs and wonders among His people, giving them abundant life and revelation for things to come and situations yet to take place, many who claim to be shepherds around the world will be proofed by the Lord as either a shepherd or a hireling.

While the great "falling away" is sad, it is also predictable. Many Christians listen to the thieves and the robbers. They believe someone or something other than Jesus. How do you prove a real shepherd, a real father and a real mother? Solomon told us. In our modern times, we know a real parent because when life gets tough, they stay, covering and protecting the children. They don't cut and run. I have a question: When will we have eyes and ears to see and hear what the Spirit is saying to the churches?

Suddenly

Isaiah 11:6-10: "The wolf also shall dwell with the lamb, and the leopard shall lie down with the kid; and the calf and the young lion and the fatling together; and a little child shall lead them. And the cow and the bear shall feed; their young ones shall lie down together: and the lion shall eat straw like the ox. And the sucking child shall play on the hole of the asp, and the weaned child shall put his hand on the cockatrice's den. They shall not hurt nor destroy in all my holy mountain: for the earth shall be full of the knowledge of the LORD, as the waters cover the sea. And in that day there shall be a root of Jesse, which shall stand for an ensign of the people; to it shall the Gentiles seek: and his rest shall be glorious."

Chapter Fourteen

Hope In A Suddenly God: A God Of Wholeness

In the previous chapters I shared quite a bit about *why* we must speak God's proclamatory words to see the effect of change in our environments within our respective countries. I'd like to share a how-type of word in this chapter. To realize the "how" we have to hear what it is that the Spirit is saying to the churches. That theme is all over the book of Revelation. This should not surprise us since the full title of the epistle is *The Revelation of Jesus Christ*. The Holy Spirit always takes from what is Christ's and shares it with the church.

When I was younger I did not enjoy public speaking. Once I realized what I was hearing was truly God, my squeamishness concerning public speaking was abated. Jesus called me with a teaching gift. It was the elders of the church who realized it and made use of it. Almost simultaneously— at least that's what it seemed like to me— I started to clearly hear messages in church meetings as if God was speaking to me privately. As I read my Bible and sat under the teaching of our pastor, I learned it was a gift of prophecy and that its purpose was to exhort, edify and comfort the church. The Lord made plain to me that He wanted me to open my mouth and speak. I asked the Lord that if He confirmed the words I was hearing in the congregation, then I would speak them. Well, He graciously granted me this request.

Suddenly

I sat silent and would watch as so many other aspects of the meeting would confirm what I felt I was hearing Him say to me. Whether it was the pulpit message, a program happening that day like a baptism, or something else, He always confirmed this word. Finally, one day He became very clear with me: "You know it is my word, now speak as I command." I didn't realize I had grown comfortable with listening but not so comfortable with speaking publicly. First, I wanted no attention drawn to myself. Secondly, what would people think?

And that's when I realized that the fear of man is the same as the sin of pride. God exposes all our hearts when He speaks. Nothing is hid before His eyes. As the years went by, that sweet little teaching gift and gift of prophecy inside the church building came with a prophetic call. Persecution, hatred from others and outright lies followed. It was during that point in time I gave up even attempting to please people. That's when He called me as a pastor. Of course, I told Him prophetic voices make lousy pastors and didn't He want to reconsider that idea? He did not.

I was always taught as a Christian to never draw attention to yourself; when we lift up Jesus, He draws all to Himself. This is totally true and is the only policy to follow. Unfortunately, He still uses people to speak. Once I got over myself and learned His voice, I became secure in speaking His words and learning how to lift up Christ. When Jesus is lifted up, all of mankind is drawn to the love of our Savior. That is the simplicity of the "how." Lift up Jesus and His love; His goodness leads all of us to repentance.

I have written a lot about God's love in this book. It is an overpowering love and a redeeming love. When we come to Him, He shows us through His love, how ugly our sin is. His love is in warning us that covenant is like gravity and spiritual rules put in place at the beginning of the planet have physical components which can play themselves out at any time we're not paying attention to them. We may not consider this "love," but it is true love. It is not a quick welfare check or a smooch behind a closed door. The check and the smooch don't always display Godly love. His love is an eternal love that has eternal consequences.

I had to get over the fact that it is in God's wisdom and love that He calls one person to ignite revival fires. I still think it's absolutely outrageous that the God who created a universe with black holes, hummingbirds, raging seas and butterflies, decides to partner with something as pitiful as human beings to spread the message of His deed of salvation. There has been more than one occasion where I wished He had used angels or something else. Even a talking dog might have more common sense than what I've witnessed in us as the human race.

And that's the rub, isn't it? He takes a fallen being, reaches out with love and kindness and leads us to repent of our sin and accept a loving Savior. What we get in the exchange is a miracle. Narcissistic human flesh exchanges for a whole new race of human being never before seen on the planet. We get to speak His life-changing word and watch whole atmospheres change. Folks who do not know Jesus intimately cannot understand this exchange. Days, weeks and months of counseling could not produce the change that one moment with our Savior produces. From selfish, uncaring imbeciles to Christ-aware, Holy Spirit-filled saints desiring to see others lifted out of the mire and helped in all areas of their lives.

People who don't understand this get it backwards. They think we resist the sin because we're just less sinful people. It has nothing to do with us. The world tells us we are psychologically impaired. But to the simple, all things are simple. All we do is say yes to what God shows us. It's that simple. As we read the Bible, He shows us how to stay away from sin by exposing the sin that's in our own hearts. He helps us to provide for our families by living and giving the faithful tithe. He shows us how to overcome by accepting His righteousness, realizing that we have none of our own: EVER! It's all Him; His grace; His suffering; His redemption and His forgiveness. All we do is accept it and learn how to function in His divine enablement. This is what Adam got wrong. It was one little mistake, but it was a doozy.

Suddenly

God always decides to separate out one or two people and use them to bring in what it is He is restoring. In this coming time period of revival, I sensed He would be using people groups to bring back what has been lost. In other words, folks who had lost healing, He would use them to bring wholeness in physical, emotional and spiritual wellbeing. Folks who had been persecuted by the church, He would use them to bring back what denominationalism has fragmented. These are just examples.

I've mentioned the Lord had been showing me things about this end-time revival long before I even knew what He was showing me. From about 1991-2005, I was studying these patterns in different sections of the Bible, when the Lord allowed me to preach for one of our former pastors. He had moved to Wisconsin and I asked the Lord what He wanted me to say. For a reason that didn't become obvious to me right away, He just kept bringing the autumn Jewish feasts before me.

Fresh Water and Former Water Combine

One in particular was the Feast of Tabernacles. It's also called the Feast of Ingathering. It was a feast where adult males traveled to the sanctuary in Jerusalem. It was a special time of music and festivity where the harvest was brought in. The sacrifices were also distinct and special during this time. It was also called the Feast of Booths owing to the lean-to type of dwellings made from branches of certain trees. This lasted for seven days. The three themes of this feast were joy or worship in music. It was dwelling in booths or out in the open nearer to God. It reminded the Israelites of their dwelling with God as they traveled from Egypt. The last theme had to do with the sacrifices, which spoke of ingathering or harvest because they had a right relationship with Jehovah.

The first day of the feast and the eighth day or what was called the Octave were holy days of rest in the Lord. No work of any kind was to be done. While the eighth day was not a part of the seven days of the Feast of Tabernacles, it was closely connected, but had an understanding of something new and different. Music was a very keen part of this feast as worship before the Lord.

Another interesting sacrifice that took place, which was similar to the mingling of the blood of the bullock and the blood of the scapegoats on the Day of Atonement was this: On the first day of the Feast of Tabernacles, the regular drink offering was taken from a golden vessel that had water drawn from the Pool of Siloam the day before. But on this day, not only that water, but fresh water from the Pool of Siloam was taken. The priest coming in with the fresh water was met with blasts of trumpets as the other water was brought in. These mingled and were poured out at the same time with wine into two separate vessels at the altar; one, for the wine the other for the waters.

That evening a celebration of lights by lit torches took place in the court of the women. It was called the "joy of the pouring out of the water." At this celebration men would dance wildly before the Lord with lit torches as the Temple shown brightly with the light of these torches. Music, trumpet blasts and hymns were sung. These ceremonies were supposed to bring to remembrance the fire by night that led the Israelites in the wilderness. The water was supposed to represent the cloud that led them by day, which was the Shechinah, or visible divine presence. This was no longer present in Herod's temple.

The congregants would recite Isaiah 12:2-3: "Behold, God is my salvation; I will trust, and will not be afraid; for the Lord God is my strength and my song, and he has become my salvation. With joy you will draw water from the wells of salvation."[47]

Levites with all sorts of musical instruments would recite the corresponding songs of ascents in the psalms.[48] On the seventh day there

---

[47] https://www.jewishencyclopedia.com/articles/14185-tabernacles-feast-of

[48] See previous and the following as both quote Babylonian Talmud, Tractate Sukkah 51a and 51b.

were prayers for salvation and on the eighth the prayer for rain.[49] It was during this time the Lord gave me the confirmation that He would be crossing the streams of revival groups; revivals that had gone on centuries before— the old water— and a new revival with fresh water, as an end-time revival. As yet, He had not told me how long it would last for.

As I sat before the Lord, preparing to go to Wisconsin, the Holy Spirit said that where I was going was the "headwaters" of our nation and that they were to seek His face for this outpouring from the Spirit. He took me to John 7:37-38:

"In the last day, that great day of the feast, Jesus stood and cried, saying, 'If any man thirst, let him come unto me, and drink. He that believeth on me, as the scripture hath said, out of his belly shall flow rivers of living water.' (But this spake he of the Spirit, which they that believe on him should receive: for the Holy Ghost was not yet given; because that Jesus was not yet glorified.) Many of the people therefore, when they heard this saying, said, Of a truth this is the Prophet. Others said, This is the Christ. But some said, Shall Christ come out of Galilee? Hath not the scripture said, That Christ cometh of the seed of David, and out of the town of Bethlehem, where David was? So there was a division among the people because of him."

I am now convinced the fresh water and the older water that was already in the pitcher could represent all the different revivals and outpourings of the Holy Spirit down through the centuries from various different church revivals, coupled with a newer, fresh outpouring. Let me also highlight some things from John's Gospel and the Feast of Ingathering.

As I studied on in John, I saw some more comparisons between what is written there and this end-time outpouring. One, Jesus equated

---

[49] https://www.oneforisrael.org/holidays/yeshua-and-the-sukkot-water-drawing-festival

freedom in the Holy Spirit, even the baptism of the Holy Spirit—evidenced by speaking with other tongues— with water. Isaiah 55:1: "Ho, every one that thirsteth, come ye to the waters, and he that hath no money; come ye, buy, and eat; yea, come, buy wine and milk without money and without price." Revelation 22:17: "The Spirit and the Bride say, 'Come.' And let the one who hears say, 'Come.' And let the one who is thirsty come; let the one who desires take the water of life without price."

It shouldn't surprise us that we read in John 7, that there was a controversy among the Jews concerning Jesus. There is a huge controversy in Christianity concerning the baptism of the Holy Spirit with the evidence of speaking with other tongues. This is one rift Father will confront in this last revival. Remember that it was during this time in the feast that light was magnificent in the Temple, especially as it emanated from the court of the women. It seemed to me as I read from different Jewish scholars at that time, that many walls of separation were lowered for that particular feast.

As we study on in John, Jesus would escape an attempted arrest by the priests, due in no small part to the wisdom of Nichodemus. So the unity didn't last long back then. In this last revival, church leaders will get cleaned up. The narcissism and corruption that we have seen in the church is another issue that will be addressed by the Lord. Those who repent will be saved. Those who continue on in their sin will not.

After this, in John 8, Jesus goes and starts teaching in the Temple again. After the light show of the previous eight days He makes this statement: "I am the light of the world. Whoever follows me will never walk in darkness, but will have the light of life" (John 8:12). It behooves us to view this statement in the light of what had just occurred.

He sits down to teach the people when the scribes and Pharisees bring Him a woman caught in adultery. We are told they have done this trying to trap Him because the Law says she should be stoned.

Suddenly

As they continue asking Him what should be done, He bends down and writes with His finger. As the scene progresses, He says to them: "He that is without sin among you, let him first cast a stone at her" (John 8:7).

We're told Jesus stooped back down and continued His doodling. Beginning from the eldest down to the youngest among them, they left, convicted by their own consciences. It's then that Jesus looks up and asks her, "Woman, where are those thine accusers? Hath no man condemned thee?" We know her answer and His proclamation of freedom: "Neither do I condemn thee: go, and sin no more" (John 8:11).

We know the devil is the accuser of the brethren. His jealousy concerning Eve is palpable. We'll study this in a minute. But for now, this time period of revival will set many women free into full-time ministry. We will see them receive the same word from Jesus as they accept His great gift of salvation: "Neither do I condemn thee…"

It doesn't take long for the Jewish leaders to regroup after the last defeat and go after Jesus again. This time their dispute is His faithful witness. The book of Revelation tells us that Jesus Christ is the faithful witness (Revelation 1:5). It begins a whole dialog about being sent as a witness. This period of outpouring will see many faithful sent out with the precious Gospel, witnessing about the faithfulness of our Lord, and bringing many souls into God's kingdom.

It will also be a time where many faithful Jews will go to their brethren and testify about Jesus, their Messiah. John 8:31-33: "Then said Jesus to those Jews which believed on him, If ye continue in my word, then are ye my disciples indeed; And ye shall know the truth, and the truth shall make you free. They answered him, We be Abraham's seed, and were never in bondage to any man: how sayest thou, Ye shall be made free?"

It's so hard for us to understand that these Jews came to an initial belief in Jesus as Messiah, but His words and ways cause the pride of the flesh to rise and bring in stumbling blocks. These are leaders, believers; but hardness of heart causes them to accuse Him of having a demon. It is precisely due to their own blinding by human deceit that satan is able to convince them that Jesus must die (John 8:34-58).

They go from belief to murder in a heartbeat when Jesus says these words, equating Himself with Ha Shem: "Jesus said unto them, 'Verily, verily, I say unto you, Before Abraham was, I am.' Then took they up stones to cast at him: but Jesus hid himself, and went out of the temple, going through the midst of them, and so passed by" (John 8:58-59).

Thereafter, we go from Jesus passing by in the midst of a murderous crowd to Chapter 9, where it opens up with this sentence: "And as Jesus passed by, he saw a man which was blind from his birth" (John 9:1). It begins a famous dialog among his disciples with Jesus concerning their erroneous theological ideas about sin and sickness. He places mud on the eyes of a man born blind. It reminds us of his doodling several verses earlier.

Many students of the Bible make much of the mud and the healing. This is one of the classic 'Messiah' miracles. But, it is what Jesus said afterwards that should catch our attention. "Go, wash in the Pool of Siloam" (John 9:7). Siloam meaning, 'sent.' Jesus would be sacrificed so that the Holy Spirit could be poured out, giving us light and life. Thereafter, we can be sent out to a lost and dying world to bring them in. Ingathering them as nations like a harvest— or guests invited to a feast— the marriage supper of the Lamb.

Lost in the dirt, mire and clay, humanity will come to be healed in this revival. They will come with odd theological ideas. They will come with prideful attitudes of where they have been and how wealthy they are and who they know or who they think they are. But they will come, and they must be confronted with a Savior that shakes them enough to dislodge the demons holding them captive to the sins of sex, lies and alibis. We must be ready to disciple many so that they can become disciples of our Lord as well. By the way, this Feast of Tabernacles is the only feast that has yet to be fulfilled.

It should not surprise us that there will be those in the religious world who will not receive an end-time revival such as this. They will kick out the revivalists from their places of worship. Many various religions will be confronted with Jesus Christ and the salvation their brethren have received. Unfortunately, the response will be similar to the one the man born blind received from the leaders in the synagogue: "They answered and said unto him, Thou wast altogether born in sins, and dost thou teach us? And they cast him out" (John 9:34). We must also be prepared to help those who will be kicked out; who become persecuted by other religions when they're found out to have received Christ, and that they now worship Him instead.

The gospel continues with many miracles and incredible promises from Jesus concerning the coming Holy Spirit, the raising of Lazarus from the dead and the persecution from the Jews. Similar circumstances as these will take place in this revival. But I need to jump to one last scene before we go to Genesis. We know that it was Mary, Martha's sister that took a pound of spikenard and wiped Jesus' feet with her hair as she anointed him with ointment for burial. Judas Iscariot makes a big deal of this, complaining that it should have been saved to feed the poor. Jesus tells him plainly that she did it for his burial and that the poor will always be with them. This is the second time Judas complains about a similar deed.

Women Displaying God's Wholeness

There are three separate instances of Jesus being anointed by a woman. The instance of Mary anointing Jesus' feet in John's Gospel, as I've just related. This took place six days before the passover when Jesus would be crucified (John 12:1-11). Then, there is the scene at Simon, the Pharisees' house where a woman comes in, washing His feet with her tears and wiping them with her hair (Luke 7:36-50). She opens an alabaster box filled with ointment and we know she begins to anoint His feet with it after she washed and kissed them.

Hope In A Suddenly God: A God Of Wholeness

This anointing is at the beginning of Jesus' ministry, sometime after He picks the twelve disciples. We know from Simon's reaction that she was a prominent sinner in the city. Jesus does not dispute this, but instead tells the story of two debtors who owed different amounts of money, one more than the other. Jesus asks Simon which man does he think will love the creditor who forgave the debts more? Simon says the one who owed more. Jesus says this, "Wherefore I say unto thee, her sins, which are many, are forgiven; for she loved much: but to whom little is forgiven, the same loveth little" (Luke 7:47). Jesus then forgives her sins and tells her that her faith has saved her.

The third and last anointing is in two different gospels: Matthew 26:6-13 and Mark 14:3-9. This woman also has an alabaster box filled with spikenard. We know it had to be broken in order for it to be used to anoint His head. We are told about these women in all four gospels. Jesus said of this woman that wherever the Gospel would be preached her deed in anointing Him for burial would be shared as a memorial of her. We also know that the disciples complained about the waste, probably spearheaded by Judas Iscariot, the keeper of the ministry purse. This took place two days before the passover where He would be arrested.

Let's look at a few things about these women who anointed the body of Jesus. We know that there were many other women that ministered to Jesus' needs while he was on earth (Luke 8:2-3). We also know that His mother and her associates ministered to Him as well, along with wealthy men (Luke 23:49-24:10). But these three women highlighted something to me concerning this end-time harvest revival. It is a harvest before the body of Christ is raptured out. Timings I know nothing about; but the concepts typifying these three are revealed to us in the Scripture. I'm going to look at them in a timeline.

We know the first woman was a sinner. She had many sins to be forgiven of and we know that she loved Jesus the more for it because He tells us so. We also know the disciples and prominent people were at the Pharisee's table. Because he was a Pharisee it is unlikely that any but Jews would have been there.

There will be many women that come out of lifestyles of sin that the church, the world over, has shunned. Because of their great love for the Savior, they will minister to the body of Christ in these last days in spite of what some think of them. Their anointing will be pure, as alabaster is white. After they repent and come to Christ, the love they have for our Savior will be a fragrant anointing for the church. Their love will teach all of us something. Many will come back to their "first love" because of these women's ministries. They will wash the body both in water and oil. They will spend whatever they have to do this, whether the church likes it or not. This will prepare the body for works of service quite early on in the revival timeline.

The next woman we know to be Mary, Martha and Lazarus' sister. She is the one who was admonished by her sister to get up and work. But she chose the better part, Jesus told us, by sitting at His feet and learning. These women will have been raised up in and around the church. They will have learned things from our Lord through prayer and worship, attending at the word and learning, as it were, at His feet. We are not told of the vessel Mary used. Instead of a vessel, I believe these women are the vessels. As a vessel or conduit for the glory, she used a whole pound of the ointment and its fragrance filled the whole house. These type of women will minister as holy vessels to the body midway and just before the end or the rapture of the church. Their ministry will fill many churches with a fragrance of notable service in music, artistic endeavors, teachings and much more. Their ministries will propel the body of Christ to be a fragrant offering in the world.

The last woman is the one with the broken vessel. Like the first woman, the vessel is pure white, but it is different. These women are not known as "sinners" but as broken. They come from all walks of life, and life has broken them. It has taken its toll. We all know people like this; you can read it in their faces. Time has not been kind. Coming closer in time to the rapture moment— this woman anoints

Hope In A Suddenly God: A God Of Wholeness

His head two days before the passover— they selflessly serve. Seemingly with no hope because of their brokenness, they will come and anoint the head. The women fitting this category will probably be more well known among their church groups, having stories and other memorials told about them. They will be used to minister to church leaders and various other ministers and Christians with necessary leadership skills. There are so many parts within a head that nobody sees, but without it being there, you don't have a body. Nobody sees our brains, but without a brain, there is no functional body.

Our first two women-types may not be as well known to their larger church communities as this last woman in our timeline, but their ministry to the body of Christ will be no less chosen and no less necessary. Complaints will be made about all of these women. They're too loud, too pricey; they're just too much dang time and effort to work with. They're too messed up; downright broken little know-it-alls, who do they think they are? Ah, but our Lord will redeem each one and give each type an anointing and word of encouragement. Each will have their assignments; some as vessels of honor and some not so notable. But all with an anointing from the Holy Spirit to wash, kiss and anoint for service the whole body of Christ.

They will have an anointing to bring wholeness back into a fractured and broken body with words of wisdom, understanding, comfort, encouragement and hope in a suddenly God.

Suddenly

Amos 9:13: "Be sure of this, the time is coming," says the Lord, "when the plowman will catch up to the reaper and the one who stomps the grapes will overtake the planter. Juice will run down the slopes, it will flow down all the hillsides" (NET Bible).

Chapter Fifteen

An Overflowing Outpouring:
Revival To First Types

Many years passed from the time of the "Headwaters" word preached in 2003-2005 in Wisconsin. During that time the Lord kept showing me different aspects of the revival that He was sending on the face of the earth.[50] I kept seeing patterns all throughout the Old Testament, but especially in Genesis. Mankind, without Christ's redemptive blood and the outpouring of the Holy Spirit is hopelessly broken. With each revival, God's redemptive pattern is to bring wholeness out of brokenness. To bring a fractured people, Israel, and a fractured mankind stemming from Adam and Eve into one New Man under Messiah: Christians and Jews, men and women, all back into the whole of the New Man, Jesus Christ. It is to prepare a bride and bring her to Him.

Headwater Revivalists

---

[50] Many years later, I called our former pastor again and related an issue I was having and he said to me that the Holy Spirit had told him to call me, but as life gets busy with all of us, he had forgotten. He told me to come on up and preach. Those four sermons morphed into the research that I had done for the book, "70 Years of American Captivity: The Polity of God, The Birth of a Nation, and The Betrayal of Government." He retired and in 2015, I had another word for the church that he started. By then it had been renamed and there were new pastors. That research that was preached in 2015, is what you will be reading in this chapter. I combine it with the "Headwater" word from the early 2000s, because that's what the Holy Spirit showed me at that time.

Suddenly

We talked about this before how God often raises up one man or woman or one couple, and by raising up that one, revival fires then spread through broader groups of people. I believe in this end-time harvest revival, we are going to see groups or types of people being used. I don't mean to imply that God will not use one man, one woman or one couple; He will. But I believe because of the length of time involved here, as well as the trouble the world will see during this period of time, He will raise up many with similar issues who can spread out to bring wholeness to various regions of the world.

The word *roshe* in Hebrew means top summit, upper part, height, beginning, chief, head of a division or company. Every river, no matter its size, must be connected to headwaters. They can be small trickles of water, but something takes place underground, quite often in unseen places or in topography above ground to enable this small body of water to become a river.

In order to sustain the rivers of revival, connection to the Head, Jesus, is vital. Believers on earth must maintain an open heaven over any church. While the heaven is open to the waters above the church, the river in the church is connected to the deep wells below, maintaining her Headwater connection to Jesus. Let us study Genesis to see where we've become broken and fractured and where we can see overflowing rivers of hope and wholeness restored in Christ.

First Principles Anointing

There is a principle in the Bible wherever something is mentioned first or created first will govern or explain everything else concerning that subject. Paul, a rabbi, said it like this when it came to understanding demonic hierarchy: We wrestle not against flesh and blood, but against principalities and powers, against rulers of the dark places or dark things on the earth. Some translations, *this present dark age*, and both are correct from the Greek. The English word *power* is the Greek word *exousia*. It means the power of choice or liberty of doing as one pleases, to have the ability or strength to rule, as in government or influence in jurisdiction; almost as a sign of that authority, like a crown.

The English word *principality* is the Greek word *arche*. Arche means the beginning or origin of a thing, that which commences it or the first place of a rule or magistracy, as in angels and demons. We have a similar understanding in Genesis. The Hebrew word for Genesis is Bereshit or Beginnings. Bereshit is different but similar to arche.

So an archetype would be the example of a first-things-first principle or train of thought. For example, Abraham is the archetype of faith-filled thought. Here in Ephesians, Paul describes the fact that satan has entities or first things, probably demonic rulers. They hold rule over the dark things in this world. That includes thought as well as practice, but especially thought or thinking patterns. It includes rulers that are in high places of worldly government. All these dynamics are seen in the Greek. But the main form of attack is to lose one's choice or to even have a choice because one's mind has been circumvented from its own ability to do as one pleases.

The amazing thing about Jesus is that He bypasses all norms. The devil demands that things be done as he is used to having them done. He was first and so this new creation represented by Adam and Eve can't have preeminence. So when Jesus comes to redeem what the devil and sinful human flesh has fragmented, He may very well take a representative of the problem and use that individual or couple to bring His redemptive purposes. But, He can very well turn all of it on its head.

Jesus said in Matthew 20:16, that the first will be last and the last, first. He is talking about the Jewish people are first and will be brought into the Kingdom last. The "goyim" or Gentiles were last, yet because of belief in Him, would be brought in first. But He is also talking about Him changing or making new firsts, so that He makes a whole new Kingdom where the "firsts" will be changed into a different understanding of what it means to be first. For example, Adam was first; now Christ is first in a whole new order of created beings.

Suddenly

Our earthly parents are first in procreating us. Now, Father God is our new parent; this also in conjunction with being birthed by the word and the Spirit.

Genesis: The Beginning of Firsts

Genesis 1:1, is the first place we see patterns. It is Bereshit, or Beginnings; scholars terming this the beginning of the first-things-first principles. So what we see here will be a pattern for what we see everywhere else. The Hebrew language is consonants. The vowels were added later. The consonants are numbers as well as giving some understanding to punctuation marks. Here we see the first patterns in the words, *"Let there be and so there was and it was good."* They really are like little exclamation points in the Hebrew. You don't quite come to the same understanding in the English. To us the punctuation is independent and governing. In the Hebrew it is all one. The words are the meaning, numbers and sometimes the punctuation.

So in Genesis we see the first patterns of the heavens and earth; patterns for the earth and the waters/sky. We see the pattern of God creating by His word— the *davar of the Lord*— as a driving force that creates something out of nothing. Ten times in the first chapter of Genesis we see the Hebrew verb *amar (to say/utter)* with the vav in front of it, translated as *said* (God *said*). We realize the verb **to be** is used as a word play with the words translated in English as "God said" and the following action of 'let there be, and so there was.' These words are like the exclamation points in the Hebrew. They are highlighted as if they were little moments of *Ta!da!Da!da!*

The word-play here calls something into being and declares its divine fulfillment with the same breath. When God does this He shows us how to speak His word from a place of intimacy with Him so we reproduce or allow the word to procreate around us. This is how Jesus did so in the New Testament because He saw His Father do so when the earth was bereshit: beginning. This is the first place Adam failed. Instead of waiting on the Lord to teach him what he needed, Adam failed to speak God's word to an infiltrating enemy and stay around

An Overflowing Outpouring: Revival To First Types

for the object lessons. Jesus does not make the same mistake, and neither should we. When God comes in revival to restore, it is to restore an intimacy where we may declare His word to the earth and see healing.

Being mindful of the patterns, we know that the heavens and earth were created first, and they will be the last thing made new. This will be far after any end-time revival occurs. In the beginning we see the pattern of God creating by His word and then we see the pattern of Him separating by that same word. For us sin has marred the beauty of Godly separation. God does not do so as we do to divide and conquer. God does so to bless. We see Him speaking/creating light and darkness into existence. This is a blessing for us to work in the light and sleep in the dark. He separates the waters so we do not have to wade in them to live; we can walk on dry land.

The difference in Godly separation is a mutual exclusivity. This idea is seen throughout the whole of the Scripture and it is meant to be a blessing. The light is not meant to curse darkness. God used the light to dispel the darkness. He does not do away with the darkness completely, but that the light comes alongside the darkness, showing mutual exclusivity.

We see where He separates clean and unclean, holy and profane. What is seen is a holy exclusivity to produce what will be beneficial. We never see separation God's way. Because of our sin nature, God has to tell Peter in Acts that there is now a change to his idea of the pattern: "Don't call unclean what I have made clean" (Acts 10:9-16; 11:1-12). It was sin that made *tamei* radioactive toxicity when we *shaatnez*, or mix our works-based actions with God's all-encompassing plans.

When God separated Israel and called her chosen, it was not to be superior or pretend to be something she was not, but to show the world the superiority of how to live in health and wholeness because the God of Israel was living among them. Israel was placed in the middle of everything to show those passing through her borders how awesome this God truly is. Instead, they desired to subjugate the people of Israel and steal the natural resources meant as a blessing for the world as Israel mined and capitalized on the resources.

When God comes in reviving glory, He brings blessing with Him to restore the separation and captivity sin has discharged into our members. When God places a nation of Christians— as in America— into a global community, it is to show others how to govern God's way in covenant. It is to show others how awesome this God is to serve. Broke, busted and disgusted is not how God wants us to live. This is how the devil wants to see mankind survive; to barely eke out life. When revival breaks out, blessing in finances, resources and creativity break out at the same time. It is impossible for that not to happen.

Naming Invokes the Blessing

In Genesis 1:5, we have another first pattern connected to God's pattern of speaking at the Bereshit. We see the pattern of God calling or naming things. When He does so, this invokes a blessing. The Hebrew understanding is that whatever God calls or names, He blesses and has *sovereignty* over it. This was another lesson God wanted to teach Adam and Eve, but sin short-circuited. Seven times in this chapter we see God naming, blessing and thus having sovereignty over something— and it was good— what God created gave Him enjoyment.

This is where we see the concept of mutual blessing first invoked. So we see another first principle pattern; one which undergirds everything else. In fact, as we go on we shall see each principle or pattern bless or undergird the former.

This pattern of mutual blessing undergirds; it is the first place we see sowing and reaping and we understand the nature of true worship. We see the Triune God in an eternal context of functioning within an interdependent and mutually beneficial relationship of Father, Son and Holy Spirit. The Hebrew gives us an understanding of God enjoying what He creates as well as depending on what He created to give Him enjoyment.

Of course, this is why when Adam sinned, God made the pronouncement that from now on it will be by the sweat of his brow he would bring forth from the earth. Instead of learning from God and declaring, Adam short-circuited the learning process. So now, he must work.

When God tells us to name our sins and repent, it's not to make us feel worse; it is to show us how to have sovereignty over something by exposing it and calling it what it is. To see how God desires a healthy principle effect here, He brings the animals of creation to Adam to name. This is so he has a healthy dominion over creation, NOT the idea we have because of sin. Adam blesses the animals in creation by naming them. What attempted to mess these principles up is Lucifer's rebellious sin.

Sin sees the animals in subjugation. God saw Adam as a caretaking sovereign representing the animal kingdom on earth to the heavenly Council, and then representing the blessing from the heavenly Council to the animal kingdom here on earth. This is before God must slay an animal to cover Adam and Eve's sin. The understanding for Adam to subdue was to harness the potential of the animal kingdom and use its resources for benefit; i.e., mutual beneficence. When God speaks, He creates, He blesses, and what is created is blessed by God and is a blessing to God. The easiest place to see this is in the New Testament in what Christians consider the beginning of Jesus coming on the scene.

John 1:1: "In the beginning was the word, and the word was with God and the word was God." The actual Greek words are *pros ton theos*. Of course, it can be translated as the word *was* God, but technically it says, the word was *toward* God. In a mutually beneficial context of trinity, to benefit each other, to bless each other: this is our God.

Suddenly

This is the very definition of worship. When God comes to restore in revival, true worship is at the forefront and is restored to mankind. Mankind gives our God worship, He receives this and blesses mankind in the process.

What God creates gives Him enjoyment, thus everything that is created benefits the next creation. Water benefits land, land is supposed to benefit water, plants benefit the earth, and earth benefits plants; animals benefit both plants and earth and sea, and earth and sea benefit them. Mankind is not supposed to worship the creation, but God. Sin sees mankind shirking his proper duty as a caretaking sovereign by worshiping the creation. Mankind is supposed to give enjoyment to God, God benefits mankind, mankind benefits the earth, sea and animals and these things benefit man. This is wholeness as God created.

Seventy: Blessing/Conception or Judgment; We Choose

God said (ten times), "Let there Be . . . and so There Was. This is the Name of It, and It was Good!" We see that seven times, and the Hebrew is like exclamation points. So we see the numeral combination of ten times seven, equalling seventy. In Christian theology ten represents human governing forces; we have ten fingers and toes, or what governs humans as in Ten Commandments. In Christian theology, seven represents an area of divine completion; the earth was finished in seven days. In Jewish theology seven would mean divine connections.

Now, the number seventy has some very interesting placements. The first time it is mentioned as a number is in Genesis 4:23, where Lamech slays unintentionally and believes judgment against him should be less than Cain's sentence. Many Jewish scholars see this as both judgment and conception because of the conversation Lamech is having with his wives.

Another time is when Jeremiah understands that Israel will go into captivity for seventy years because of her rebellion. But we see other

An Overflowing Outpouring: Revival To First Types

connections for the number seventy where God uses it as a blessing, as He did in creation. In the Hebrew language the word *wine* has the number seventy as its denominator. The word *eye* also has a similar denomination.

In Jewish theology, the right eye is for viewing others, discerning spiritual insight, but the left eye is for judging, for internal review and understanding. Both of them together bring a unified vision for spiritual as well as physical judgment or interpretation.[51] These various viewpoints may very well be the reason why seventy was viewed as both judgment and blessing.

One of the most significant connections for the number seventy is in the concepts seen in the words *source, well, spring, fountain* or *origin*. These would be because of God creating: *let there be*. What He did when He created: *and so there was*. And what He said about it: *and it was good*. These are just a few connections we see with the number. Blessing is in the original intention from God; judgment only occurred when we refuse Godly instruction.

So when God comes in restoration revival, earthly or mankind-involved national governing structures must be cleansed of the interloping, lying enemies who infiltrate these structures. No end-time revival will be political; nevertheless, politics may have no choice but to change. With a revival this many years' long, some nations will change quickly, while others will take some time, especially in entrenched communistic systems. Of course, the first change in human governing systems will be seen within the true church. No man knows the day or the time or the hour of all these things, but the book of Revelation does make plain that no change can ever be seen in any one-world governing system. That thing will be corrupt until the end, when God brings everything to a conclusion.

I don't want to ignore the patterns in the Jewish reckoning of time. We see how evening came and then the morning. We see night and

---

[51] https://www.betemunah.org/seventy.html

Suddenly

then there was day: Six days to work and on the seventh Shabbat (Sabbath) rest! The writer of the book of Hebrews tells us that there is a Sabbath rest for all those who hear His voice and do not harden their hearts. All who accept Christ's work, rest from their own in His gift of salvation. The burden of night and then day and then work will be made new so wholeness is reproduced, not dread and weariness.

I can personally attest to Father coming in glory in my home and losing the day in Him. I vaguely remember it being mid-morning when I saw the first vision. All sense of earthly time vanished, until God allowed it to invade my time and space again. I was never asleep, I was just seeing what God wanted me to see in vision form as the Ancient of Days came into my living room. When I 'snapped' out of it, I found out hours and hours had passed. The day was literally gone; yet, it seemed like mere moments to me. Because of missing critical appointments that afternoon, I realized that experience shifted where my life was going and put me on a whole different path.

Adam lost the idyllic nature of Godly enterprising rest when sin became part of his members. God brings us back in time to restore what has been lost in time so we rest from our labors and work in His Kingdom. Some of these first types will receive the benefit from revival last and others will be first. In all these areas we should be able to see how any long-term revival will bring restoration to what has been fractured, compromised and broken.

Obviously, deliverance from demonic forces will be important in any end-time revival. But I don't want to leave the impression that all things can be impacted. Many await the fulfillment of time in what our Lord has already proclaimed. For instance, some things can never be affected as we understand it, like the devil and his entourage being thrown in the Lake of Fire. That act by God will foreshadow a new heaven and new earth (Revelation 20:10-11). By then, the Bride of Christ will have long left revivals; faith having become sight.

Suddenly

Ephesians 1:15-23: "*Wherefore I also, after I heard of your faith in the Lord Jesus, and love unto all the saints, Cease not to give thanks for you, making mention of you in my prayers; That the God of our Lord Jesus Christ, the Father of glory, may give unto you the spirit of wisdom and revelation in the knowledge of him: The eyes of your understanding being enlightened; that ye may know what is the hope of his calling, and what the riches of the glory of his inheritance in the saints, And what is the exceeding greatness of his power to us-ward who believe, according to the working of his mighty power, Which he wrought in Christ, when he raised him from the dead, and set him at his own right hand in the heavenly places, Far above all principality, and power, and might, and dominion, and every name that is named, not only in this world, but also in that which is to come: And hath put all things under his feet, and gave him to be the head over all things to the church, Which is his body, the fulness of him that filleth all in all.*"

Chapter Sixteen

Outpouring: Mankind

Another exclamation point from the Hebrew in Genesis is the creation of man. Adam means both humankind and man. The understanding is that mankind— both male and female— are endowed with a capacity to represent the image of God to His heavenly court as a just ruler, both in spiritual matters and physical ones.

Genesis 2:7: The Lord God formed— Hebrew word, *yatsar*— it means to fashion, usually by design and plan. This word for *formed* relates exactly to a similar Hebrew word *yotser*. Yotser refers to an artist's work. "And Yahveh God formed the man— soil, from the ground. And breathed into his nostrils the breath of life." This term is used for God imparting life to humans, not animals. It conveys more than breathing. Whatever has this breath becomes animated with life from God in a functioning conscience with spiritual understanding (Proverbs 20:27). It's where we get our divine image from.

The man became a living being. Both animals and humankind are described in the Hebrew as living beings, but mankind became different because the body came from the soil but the breath came from God. The Hebrew is usually translated soul, but the word frequently refers to the **whole person.** The divine image does more than just relate man to God in familial unity. This divine image is what gives mankind the capacity to represent God and His heavenly court as a pattern on earth. Sin destroyed this representation.

Sin also destroys God's originally created design in Adam to pass on His image in reproduction. Jesus restored it anew with a New Covenant. Christ gives us the ability to reproduce in a whole new dimension. The Greek word *parousia* describes how Christ *came* to heal us. It also describes Christ arriving and constantly *coming* to be reproduced in the hearts and minds of our fellow Adam or mankind as we share the Gospel message. I've often joked that I can hear God calling to Adam in the cool of the garden, "Soil, Soil . . . *Dirt!* Where are you?" It should remind all of us the price Christ paid to buy us back from a dirt-filled grave.

What many ignore is that Eve's creating is no less miraculous. The Hebrew is also revealing in this vignette. God says, "I will make a companion for him who corresponds to him." The literal translation could read "according to the opposite of him." The idea from the Hebrew is that God creates everything in the woman that the man needs and he created everything in the man that the woman needs. They would each supply whatever was lacking in the other's design.

This is more than in the physical realm. It relates on every plane of humankind: in our spirits, our souls and our bodies. They would not be able to do what they are designed to do without the other. These words are not used to describe anyone else other than the male-female marriage relationship, except God. Intimacy with God or the male-female marriage relationship is the only way we fulfill our destinies within our life times. Our marriage relationship and/or our relationship to our Creator produces a wholeness to reproduce. Wholeness is critically important to God. I would say it is the crux of why the creation story is revealed. God created in wholeness and something happened to fracture this wholeness.

So God comes in revival to restore and make whole again. Male and female relationships on this planet are hopelessly broken. When God comes in revival fires, He restores Eve to her place in sovereignty alongside Adam. Many of the church teachings place woman as a doormat, unable to apply proper theology to a marriage relationship, never mind as leadership within the body of Christ.

Submission in Wholeness, Not Subjugation

Paul tells us that wives are to submit to their husbands and that husbands are to die for their wives. It goes beyond some church leaders' heads that they only have one wife in the church. The whole body is to submit in Godly wholeness to one another. We still have a hard time understanding healthy submission as it relates to divine wholeness. All we see and understand is subjugation, which eventually brings subversion. Subjugation means the action of bringing someone or something under domination or control. The noun, subversion, is the undermining of the power and authority of an established system or institution.

I've seen some of the most demonic teachings on submission in the church. They are some of the church's best selling book/study guides. They reproduce two things. The first is a corralling of the body of Christ to be obedient to the leadership of a church: The definition meaning to be good, little Christians who sit on pews and utter sweet nothings to God; never questioning authority and never doing anything of import for the cause of Christ. If you do, you will be seen as a usurper, attempting to minister in place of the authorized leadership.

When you peel away the fancy videos, slick book and study guides accompanying these fantasies which claim biblical inspiration, they are nothing more than desires to subvert the body of Christ under the teachings of complacency. This subversion will neuter any Holy Spirit-inspired ministry within the body to go out into the streets to bring in the harvest of lost souls.

They do something else: they put the cart before the horse. What do I mean by that? Very rarely do these teachings start off with what classic, New Testament leadership should look like. I mean, if you're going to claim a people group submit to leaders at all cost, what does a leader look like, from God's perspective? The second thing these teachings do is reproduce a marriage where the wife is a child and the husband rules as king. It's a wonder she can even cook, shop or take care of children.

Godly Submission: The Love Quotient

The New Testament repeatedly tells us to submit. One of the classic Scriptures is from James 4:7: "Submit yourselves therefore to God. Resist the devil, and he will flee from you." Another important passage is from Ephesians 5:21-6:9, where Paul tells the church worldwide to submit. He tells wives, husbands, children, fathers, employees and employers to submit, one to another. His parameter for such Christian submission? Love; love for the saints, for the family, for each other, and above all, our love for Jesus.

All church and Christian families are governed by love. Inherent in Christian church governing documents is the understanding of love. Our governmental language is love, but it is fleshed out through the understanding of our New Testament Covenant. This covenant is based on the sacrifice and blood of Jesus. The attitude which should be present from leadership and among the brethren is one of family. You would never look upon your family with unclean eyes or with disrespect or with attitudes of superiority.

The problem today is we have lost the valuable language of love as well as the life-sustaining principle of covenant. This is true whether it is among church brethren or between a husband and wife. The attitudes of superiority, disrespect and unclean eyes may never be realized; yet, it is what many church teachings on submission become when fleshed out.

Let's look at Romans 12:1-3: "I beseech you therefore, brethren, by the mercies of God, that ye present your bodies a living sacrifice, holy, acceptable unto God, which is your reasonable service." There is no greater level of submission than to present our bodies as living sacrifices to our Lord. This is the first example of submission for any Christian, whether one wishes to claim leadership or not. I would present this as my first rebuttal to any subversive teaching on submission. Christians are to present their bodies before the Lord. For leaders to assume that means the body is to be presented to them, is apostasy. What do I mean when I say this?

We are called to learn Christ under the tutelage of good, Christian leaders. They are called the elders of the church for a reason. This is called discipleship, which we will talk about shortly. This is proper and appropriate submission to those in authority who care for our souls. But to assume that the people "belong" to us as leaders is, again, backward thinking. Even when we are in correct relationship to our Christian leadership, the body belongs to Christ. Leadership become under-shepherds, under our Great High Shepherd, Jesus Christ. Our desire is to so care for the sheep that they are presented as holy before our Lord.

Remember my understanding from Jesus that His holiness brings total wholeness. Leadership's attitude must be a willingness to die for the body in order to see them discipled unto the things of Christ, which will reproduce wholeness in their members. They will be able to stand before Jesus on that Day, not lacking in anything. At the very least not lacking due to their shepherds' discipling them concerning the things of Christ with care and brother-sisterly love.

Leadership can reproduce good, as well as bad character attributes in the people they minister to. So what can remove bad character traits or attributes affecting Jesus' bride? Submission to Jesus, to the point of death, is the definitive word termed *sacrifice* that weeds out the dross. When we view the body of Christ from a New Testament standard, we see all the early leadership, as well as all the apostles— in fact, the entire body of Christ— presenting themselves as sacrifices in the torture chambers of the gladiator games within the Roman era.

Persecution and martyrdom are great equalizers. If you've looked at some of these teachings on submission making the circuit today in some churches and compare them to the early church's dynamics, they make no sense. From this standard of the first century church, a good portion of our American, Christian church leaders are backslidden. I'm going to use the example of the American church as a harbinger of what God does when He sends an outpouring to heal our rifts, fragmentation and brokenness. Before we view the American church, let's look at the marriage relationship in light of some of these teachings.

Realizing Godly Wholeness Inside Marriages

Husbands are commanded to be like Jesus; so much so, that they give their lives for their wives. I have seen teachings today within some churches that make wives barely any more than sex slaves. Even when that's not the practice, the end result of these submission teachings reproduce that attitude. Does this seem like the relationship between Christ and His bride? It does not. This is the definition of abuse and narcissism (2 Timothy 3:2). The definition of a narcissist is the excessive interest in, or admiration of, oneself and one's physical appearance. The definition of narcissism is selfishness, involving a sense of entitlement, a lack of empathy, and a need for admiration, as characterizing a personality type (2 Timothy 3:3-5).

What attracted me to my husband was first visual. As humans we are designed this way. But that first attraction must go beyond that. I next saw a holiness and reverence for Jesus. I then realized this man loved me to the point of dying for me. He cherished me, even adoring me. That reproduced more than a respect for him. It gave me a desire to honor him. I realized what a gift he was from Jesus to me. He realized that I was a gift from Jesus to him. We became mutually submitted to one another, even though we realized he had a much deeper responsibility in caring for me and our family. Our pastor taught us his responsibilities from Christ and taught us mine, especially in light of Proverbs 31.

Outpouring: Mankind

Our engagement was long: about a year and a quarter. Did we have to work out areas of our flesh that did not align to the Gospel message and language of love? Yes, we did. We are still human; tempers can flare and attitudes need to go to the cross. But the one thing my husband never did was treat me with disrespect, or as incompetent and unable to succeed. We knew each one possessed different leadership skills. In fact, as we sat before our pastor for premarital counseling, he told us so. He gave us great words of wisdom: Let Jesus show you what skills you each possess and each one of you do them to the best of your ability to further the destiny call of Christ that you have as a family.

As we got older and had to move on to other church families, I realized how blessed I was to have the husband I had. What I saw among many marriages was more control and manipulation. It shocked me and I couldn't understand how these personality traits had gained such a foothold in the body of Christ. How do I know many church teachings on submission are in error? Let's look at what's being reproduced.

Reproduction

According to Barna, almost half of practicing Christian millennials believe it is wrong to evangelize.[52] Frankly, I was floored when I read that. Sharing Jesus, whether as individuals, couples, families or church ministries is the only way to reproduce Christ on the earth. The cornerstone and, in my opinion, the only way to prevent demons and other religious spirits from infecting a church is to have a Holy Spirit-led evangelization outreach up and running within a congregation. This is where people are taught how to share Jesus.

Notice I didn't say share your faith, but to share Jesus. This is where we fail. We want to share our church; we want to share our love for Jesus, thus subtly making it about us. That is the end result of narcissism. We can't even tell when we're acting like narcissists. If we're

---

[52] https://www.barna.com/research/millennials-oppose-evangelism/

not bragging about the numbers we're seeing saved, we're bragging about something else. Please don't misunderstand me. We must share the numbers we are seeing redeemed. It is crucial for leadership and the saints to share what folks the congregation saw impacted for the week, or who was touched with spiritual gifts, whether healing or finances or something else. Whether a congregation does this weekly or monthly does not matter.

What this does do is encourage the saints, and it lets the body and the elders know they are on the right track with the Holy Spirit in their outreach programs. It magnifies what Jesus is doing and when we do that, we draw all people to Him. I'm speaking instead about the subtle shift that can take place if we are not careful where we make everything about us.

The American Church: Converts vs. Disciples

I understand this must be a personal journey. If we are being taught to go to the cross daily, and we are being shown by example how to be led by the Holy Spirit, His fire purifies our impurities. But I had to wonder about these millennials who falsely believe evangelism is wrong. They are the next generation of leadership, if they're not in that place already. That attitude is the epitome of apostasy. It is evidence of a lack of submission to Jesus. But, it is a perfect example of submitting to human leadership which also doesn't do what our Lord says. Remember, leadership has the potential to reproduce good ideas, bad ideas, characteristics and attitudes within a congregation.

It's also a perfect result of our next area of apostasy in the American church. How did these millennials get this basic doctrinal understanding so wrong? We convert but we don't disciple and we don't disciple according to New Testament standards. Converts won't fall in love with Jesus. They may follow Him. Possibly even try to do what He instructs. But they will never have a deep and abiding relationship with the Holy Spirit, which is the next step in a relationship with Jesus when you disciple people.[53]

The early church had a first lesson of discipleship. It is seen in Hebrews 6:1-3. This is what the writer to the Hebrew believers wrote: "Therefore leaving the principles of the doctrine of Christ, let us go on unto perfection; not laying again the foundation of repentance from dead works, and of faith toward God, of the doctrine of baptisms, and of laying on of hands, and of resurrection of the dead, and of eternal judgment. And this will we do, if God permit."

From what we read, this writer is wanting to go forward in their discipleship, not go back in studying the first or foundational principles. What are those? The first is repentance from dead works. Can you remember being taught that you must flee your desires for doing things your way, and instead take on how the Holy Spirit does things? The next is faith toward God. Can you remember when you realized that you didn't have to do all the work in a church? Do you remember when it dawned on you that Jesus is quite capable of caring for His creation, without your help?

The next is baptisms; notice the plural ending. What did you learn about water baptism? Have you received the baptism of the Holy Spirit with the evidence of speaking with other tongues since you first believed? This was not an option for the early church. It's also not one for us either. Were you ever taught about the baptism of fire? I have to ask these questions because I know many weren't even baptized in water since they believed as an adult.

The next is the doctrine of the laying on of hands. How do I know we don't disciple properly in this area? Have you seen the explosion of child molestation in the church? Do you know how often 'Spouse

---

[53] Conversion doesn't work, only discipleship works, as viewed by this alarming statistic. According to Pew Research, Christianity loses more people than it gains from religious conversion. It found that 23% of Americans raised as Christians no longer identified with Christianity, whereas 6% of current Christians were converts.

Suddenly

X' wants someone else's 'Spouse Y' and off they go in an affair? If we viewed one another as brethren— family— we may finally understand why it is wrong to covet another's family or spouse.

Jesus: "You heard it was said, 'Do not commit adultery,' but I say to you that everyone who looks at a woman/wife (same Greek word) in order to covet her has already committed adultery with her in his heart" (Matthew 5:27-28). The problem here is in the action of coveting or action of seducing to get what is not lawfully yours. Seduction or grooming people or manipulating them to do something is the problem. Grooming victims is a molester's habit. By the way, this is also a hallmark of narcissism. If we would disciple concerning the parameters of the proper laying on of hands, I dare say we wouldn't see molestation, abuse and adultery by church leaders, either.

If we understood the resurrection of the dead and what eternal judgment looks like, from a New Testament perspective, many of those who aren't sure about their salvation would finally get some answers. These are all first steps in any discipleship program in a church. I don't have the space to go in depth concerning them (Hebrews 6:1-3). There are many other aspects to discipleship, like intercessory prayer, moving in the gifts of the Holy Spirit, as well as making new disciples as you lead others to Christ.

We've been told in the New Testament not to put a novice in charge of anything (1 Timothy 3:6). I didn't learn prayer firstly by a discipleship class. I learned as I went to prayer meetings and listened to the church mothers and fathers intercede in the Holy Ghost. Frankly, I've talked to young Christians who have never been taught the doctrine of the Trinity, let alone principles laid down by the early church elders of the first through fourth centuries. I don't have the time and space right now to go into hearing the voice of God, casting out demons or other areas of sanctification and transformation for the Christian. These are all places where we disciple unto the things of Christ.

Outpouring: Mankind

Let me ask one last question concerning false teachings surrounding submission. Are these teachings just a dressed-up ruse created to subvert a fiery Holy Spirit-filled church? Are they a distraction, taking our time away from evangelism and discipleship? Will the result of some of these lopsided teachings give birth to an apostate, reprobate church, reproducing blind leaders of the blind? According to Jesus, they will both fall into a ditch. Looking at our declining numbers today in American Christianity and church attendance, I'd say that's already been done.

I don't want to ignore what a real Holy Spirit-led church looks like. By the way, it has nothing to do with its size of building or numbers of people. The true bride of Christ is alive and well today. It is true that she may be in other parts of the world, but there are embers growing in America.

Holy Spirit Filled Wholeness

She looks like a church where you don't have to preach submission because the love of Christ is so evident among the saints that they would never dream of causing division and strife to get their own way. She looks like a church where humility from the Holy Spirit is evident and the saints wouldn't harm leadership or each other through gossip, rancor or immorality. She looks like a church discipling folks concerning healthy evangelism, not a works mentality.

She looks like a church where worship is vibrant and the love of the leaders is so evident that you know they would die for the Gospel, while giving their lives for the perfecting of the saints. Each gives of themselves without broadcasting it. They just do the work of Christ with humility and love. She also looks like a church where you're not exhausted by doing good works, because the very Holy Spirit of God refreshes and keeps you healthy and moving forward.

These churches and leaders have made healing, signs and wonders all about Jesus. Remember, these things are a sign of correct Gospel preaching, not a sign of leadership perfection. Mark 16:20: "And they went forth, and preached every where, the Lord working with them, and confirming the word with signs following. Amen."

Saints moving in signs and wonders, which would entail miracles, healings as well as other Holy Spirit-ordained occurrences, are not a seal that we are perfect Christians. Signs and wonders confirm the Gospel message. All Christians must die to self, taking on the character and nature of Christ. The Holy Spirit is here on earth to help us do that. By the way, repentance is the only way to accomplish that.

Leadership is made such to work as the Holy Spirit directs in order to perfect the bride of Christ; to present her as holy, blameless and spotless on the last day (2 Corinthians 11:2; Ephesians 5:27; Revelation 19:7). No leader is perfect. We are all as flawed as the next human. But leaders who make it all about Jesus are those who understand human frailty because they live it and can help everyone else overcome it through the testimony and the blood of the Lamb.

"And they overcame him by the blood of the Lamb, and by the word of their testimony; and they loved not their lives unto the death" (Revelation 12:11).

You never even have to give submission a thought in those churches because the desire of the Holy Spirit envelopes those places. The God of glory delights and sings over His people in those places. The love of the risen Christ is palpable within their midst. The joy in sharing Jesus to a lost and dying world (neighborhood) is infectious. Moving in deliverance, signs and wonders propels the saints forward to continue to want to get closer to the Lord who is confirming their preaching with signs following. And the righteous of the Lord say so in those places. This is what healthy submission looks like, and you don't need to buy a new-fangled book on submission to explain it.

You also don't have to be perfect for God to move in revival among the churches, among our marriages and among our families and communities. He wants to bring us into wholeness. His outpouring must bring things back into harmony with His holiness. When He

Outpouring: Mankind

comes in glory, He exposes narcissistic traits within us. These character issues are the personalities of demons. That's one of the reasons why many revivals became hallmarks of deliverance ministries. These demonic thieves desire to instill their nature in human flesh.

When we are in proper submission, we want our personalities and characteristics to mirror the Holy Spirit within us, who speaks of who Jesus is. We desire His glory to overcome us because we know we are but dust and need Him in every area of where we walk. He made mankind for fellowship in Genesis. Jesus died to bring us back to intimacy with His Father. When Father releases this end-time revival, His presence will remove things we do not realize are hindering intimacy. When Father releases this end-time revival, intimacy is restored in ways that encourages wholeness. The Spirit and the Bride say, Come!

Suddenly

Psalm 46:4-5: "*There is a river, the streams whereof shall make glad the city of God, the holy place of the tabernacles of the most High. God is in the midst of her; she shall not be moved: God shall help her, and that right early.*"

Revelation 22:1-2; 22:17: "*And he shewed me a pure river of water of life, clear as crystal, proceeding out of the throne of God and of the Lamb. In the midst of the street of it, and on either side of the river, was there the tree of life, which bare twelve manner of fruits, and yielded her fruit every month: and the leaves of the tree were for the healing of the nations.*" "*And the Spirit and the bride say, Come. And let him that heareth say, Come. And let him that is athirst come. And whosoever will, let him take the water of life freely.*"

Chapter Seventeen

Headwaters And The Bride

The word *sod* in Hebrew has a seventy denominator to it as well as the other words we looked at previously. The word means secret, hidden or mystery. All throughout the Hebrew nation, things were kept hidden. Not necessarily because that was God's intent, but because mankind could not understand what He was doing at the time. Or, because Messiah had not yet been sacrificed and man would have polluted what was needed to be kept clean.

Jerusalem is a good example of this. In ancient times it was separated by a wall. Within Jerusalem was the Temple, also separated except for those Jews who could pass. Within the Temple would have been the Holy Place as well as the Holy of Holies. These would be kept separated or hidden to the priests only, or one High Priest who would have been allowed in to perform the duties required.

Paul speaks about the mystery of Christ and the church, His bride (Ephesians 3:1-13). Paul spoke of the mystery of the bride arising to meet Jesus in the air (Corinthians 15). The rabbis talk about seventy as a conception belief and marriage as a hidden or secret intimacy with a 'seventy' denominator to it also. They even go as far as to point out that when God's wife, or the whole nation of Israel was born, it was in the seventieth year of Terah, Abraham's father. They make that connection because that was the year in which Abraham was born. They also point out that the covenant was cut in Abraham's seventieth year of life.[54]

Until Jesus broke down the wall of partition between Jew and Gentile and made us one new man, sin would continue our disunity (Ephesians 2:11-22). Jesus paid for the sin that kept unity hidden. Any end-time revival, as it continues in time, will bring unity so the walls are brought down. Christ is glorified in the eyes of all His people; revealed, as it were and no longer hidden. God hides nothing from us because He has revealed all to us by Christ's appearance and sacrifice for us.

Remember that wine has a seventy denominator. New wine will be unleashed and the rivers of God will flow to the healing of the nations, which at that time numbered seventy. While no end-time revival can completely accomplish those goals until we see a new heaven and earth, it will reinforce them, giving weight through revelation, signs and wonders to those Godly goals, at His appointed time.

Headwaters and the Toledoth of Genesis

Water: a life sustaining force, impossible to live without, yet able to destroy in a heartbeat. This is not how water was intended to function by God in the beginning. We come to a special place in Genesis that introduces an unusual linguistic structure. It has not been well translated in English Bibles. That's because it's not easily translated into English. I note twelve times in the book of Genesis we see this pattern of using a Hebrew noun which connects to a verb, *yalad*, meaning to bear or generate. Modern Jewish scholars view it as the word *history* when seeing the phrase *'this is what became of.'* Older English translations call it the *'generations of'* because of the verb's connection to begetting or generating.

The word is *toledot* in Hebrew. There are eleven in the book of Genesis with the first being different. In my opinion, it comprises two,

---

[54] < https://www.betemunah.org/seventy.html >

thus making twelve within Genesis.[55] I'm no scholar and to that I'd probably hear a lot of scholars in Hebrew and Genesis say, *amen!* Nevertheless, beyond being a break in the texts of ancient clay tablets, and these *toledoth* displaying this break, I see something a little more.

I've always been struck by the Lord's word that He tells the end from the beginning (Isaiah 46:10). I've often felt there is a pattern in Genesis where we see similar patterns in other biblical books that talk about the end of the age. Many of the things we lost in Genesis, we see a promise to restore in some form within other books of the Bible. This includes the book of Revelation. You can read Acts 3:19-21 as an example.

While the other toledoth are like little headlines, telling us what became of what God created, the first is divided. I read from the Masoretic text when I need to view Hebrew. It seems that without saying it in the first toledot, the suggestion is that God created, it became *something* and then it brought forth *something*. So I see the first understanding as belonging to God. Almost like having an Elijah seat or cup at the table during Passover. It is a respect of silent mention, and then the heavens and the earth generated something.

The other toledoth in Genesis are also headlines which describe what Adam, Noah, Terah (Abraham's father), Ishmael, et cetera, brought forth. I've often felt it was interesting how the first and second toledot let us know God created and something happened with

---

[55] < https://www.kolbecenter.org/the-mosaic-authorship-of-genesis-or-how-moses-wrote-genesis/ >< http://faculty.gordon.edu/hu/bi/ted_hildebrandt/ote-sources/01-genesis/text/articles-books/woudstra_gentoledot_ctj.pdf >

water and a garden and two specific trees; in other words, the heavens and the earth.[56]

Throughout Genesis we see the pattern of God blessing, naming and then we see the subject matter of this was named 'that' and then this is what became of 'that.' We see how God reproduced in holiness and then we see the deterioration because sin entered the world. The pattern of *what became of,* or what is termed by the word toledot as a heading, are major headlines in the story's narrative.[57]

We know what became of the heavens, what became of the earth and what became of mankind. Within these major headlines describe the headwaters of the earth. They flowed from the orchard Eden, or east of Eden: the place of pleasure. This housed the tree that gave life when one ate from its fruit. It also housed the other tree, which when its fruit was eaten had the ability to change human nature.

We talked about headwaters before. They don't look like much in the natural. They can form from mountains meeting, or from small typographies on or under the ground. It has always been amazing to me how they form rivers. From the word head (roshe), these first waters are small, insignificant areas of stream, sometimes present only during ice melt; yet, they can cause a mighty river. Before sin, we are told water came up from under the ground and gave life to every-

---

[56] I can't seem to find any scholars thinking out loud with the same thought I've had that the first toledot is separated, one for God and the other for heaven and earth. Now, they might have existed in my volume of research at one time, but I cannot seem to find any now. I did come across what was an article from the NET Bible folks. But that research was over six years ago, and I simply can't remember if they mentioned any similar thoughts.

[57] My practice in sharing what the Lord is showing me is to search out if anyone else has seen the same thing. I then make a footnote. I did try to track down the twelve toledot theory for this book, but couldn't find any. It's quite possible others saw it as well all those years back, but I can't find those sources now. If or when I find those scholars, I will attempt to make note of them.

thing around it. This is what watered the two trees. Once sin enters the picture something else forms the headwaters.

One of the most significant formations that create headwaters after the Adamic sin event are called escarpments. In the natural, we're told these form from two different processes. One is through fault action underground that push material above ground, thereby causing these jagged cliffs jutting up out of mountainous terrain. The other is erosion from water flooding.

There is a consensus from both biblical scholars and geology majors that the cataclysmic effect of significant flood events expose the earth's crust to the waters, causing normally unseen escarpments to jut up above the ground and mountains. This changes headwater regions, thus changing the dynamics of rivers. It can make new rivers and dry up old rivers.

Love, Water, Word and the Spirit of God

The lands that house these earthbound phenomenon are rich in mineral and other resources. Quite often the water and rock mineral in the soil produce rich and fertile lands, while in other instances the minerals are for mining. The rivers carry traces of the mineral elements downstream to fertilize and help the land many miles away from the exact location where the headwaters originate. I find it interesting how the Holy Spirit flows through mankind— Adam, soil— and thereby blessing can be seen to flow to mankind elsewhere.

Within the Genesis account we see the Hebrew word for water change from the deep, primordial type of flow to clean, crisp water. It says God piled up in heaps the water in order to separate water from land. Later in the stories of Moses and Joshua we see God do something similar to save His people. The prophets Elijah and Elisha both have experiences with parting water. In both the Old and New Testaments water becomes synonymous with the Holy Spirit, the word of God and salvation (John 4: 14; 7:37-39; Isaiah 44:3; 1

Suddenly

Corinthians 12:13; Ephesians 5:26-27; Isaiah 12:3). There are many references for Godly life and water in the Bible.

Some make God's word out to be an ethereal mist-like supernatural event. Maybe that's because of how frequently God's word is connected with water. Maybe it's because *davar*, the Hebrew for word, literally means to make something out of nothing. Frankly, God's purpose is far more grounded with a working-man's function in mind. Hebrews 13:8 says that Jesus Christ— the word made flesh (John 1)— is said to be the same yesterday, today and forever. So what aspect of God's word would carry such weight for God as to affect our yesterdays, our to-days and our forevers? It is the creative aspect of God's word that does so.

Whether God is speaking His word to make something out of nothing to create the world, or speaking a promise to your heart; He is creating a new reality for us all. This falls in line with His eternal being and nature as well as His eternal plans and purposes. Each revival brings a new aspect or understanding from the word of God that we can hold on to.

When connected with the Holy Spirit, these revivals restore the gifts of the Spirit. They encourage the saints to press on in receiving a promise or change for the earth in our own communities. I'm reminded of the restoration of the gifts of the Holy Spirit during the revivals in the 1940s through the 1960s. We were lacking one thing then that I believe will need restoration in any end-time revival, and that is a restoration within mankind's understanding of the love of God.

In 1 Corinthians 12-14, we see explanations and functioning parameters for the gifts of the Holy Spirit. Chapter 13 is sandwiched in between the two. That is not by accident. It is the love chapter. It is classic and full of poetry. It is also the only way the word of God works with the Holy Spirit in conjunction with us and the gifts. We sometimes forget that it was through the word of God that God's love for us and His creation became known. Without the revelatory word of God, His love for us never would have been known.

I believe any end-time revival will segue from a profound understanding of God's love to an understanding of the marriage supper of the Lamb. That word of God and the overriding presence of the Holy Spirit will reproduce a wooing and call for salvation. When folks accept Jesus, men and women are restored. Families are restored and marriages will be restored. It's the rivers that bring nutrition to ground many miles downstream. As rivers cut through soil, health is restored.

We have not had any major revival highlight marriages or the marriage supper of the Lamb, or women in general. It was Adam's own marriage which was interrupted by a creature so evil that it is sometimes hard for us as humans to comprehend. We see his depravity everywhere around us, but for some reason we don't acknowledge it, or deal with getting rid of its effects, effectively.

As mentioned before, the first toledoth seen within Genesis have to do with the heavens and earth and what happened with them. I've often had a hard time parsing out from the Hebrew whether the water was what produced cleanliness for the trees and that enabled the tree of life, or was it inherent in the tree? From my reading of the text, it's both. I've lived in many different parts of the United States and we often have a joke that what makes people different is what's in the water. But in the case of water before the Fall, it was no joke. There really was something in the water that sustained life in such a way as to make things grow in ways we do not see now.

Lucifer and Mankind's Wounding

We know when sin took place the earth was thrown into chaos. We know that chaos was from below ground and we know it infused the entire earth, from the ground up. We're told that something took place to change how water fed the earth. We also know Lucifer had a dual anointing. We know that his jealousy concerning Adam was two-

Suddenly

fold: It was in how Adam was created and how he functioned. We know Lucifer thought quite highly of himself and that he had some inkling due to Adam's gifts from God that he would become irrelevant. So attacking this new creation became paramount for him.

Ezekiel 28:13-16: "Thou hast been in Eden the garden of God; every precious stone was thy covering, the sardius, topaz, and the diamond, the beryl, the onyx, and the jasper, the sapphire, the emerald, and the carbuncle, and gold: the workmanship of thy tabrets and of thy pipes was prepared in thee in the day that thou wast created. Thou art the anointed cherub that covereth; and I have set thee so: thou wast upon the holy mountain of God; thou hast walked up and down in the midst of the stones of fire. Thou wast perfect in thy ways from the day that thou wast created, till iniquity was found in thee. By the multitude of thy merchandise they have filled the midst of thee with violence, and thou hast sinned: therefore I will cast thee as profane out of the mountain of God: and I will destroy thee, O covering cherub, from the midst of the stones of fire."

In Ezekiel 28, the writer gives us a description of how beautiful the Lord made Lucifer. It seems from the description that he was a living, fiery, breathing figurative gem with adornments that echoed and sang God's praise. One of the words that lets us know this is the Hebrew word *neqeb*. It is translated as pipes in the King James Version and bezel in most other translations. I believe there is a reason why the King James translators use the word pipes instead of bezel. When used in this passage, think of this word as describing a large, plain gold, wedding band that holds a gem as it blows sound through it. That 'breath' resonates light through the gem so brilliant, almost fired-color essences stream in many directions.

Remember that the prophets were trying to describe what they saw in a heavenly realm through earthly terminology. That terminology is based on the Hebrew. In this case we are fortunate because the Hebrew language is like a tree or large body of water with many roots or tributaries. As God breathes and it is released in the earth by this language, He yields it as a sharp, dazzling diamond— almost like a dual-edged sword— exposing all sides of a situation. Now, try to stay with me as I go through some of the tributaries of this word.

Neqeb comes from the word *naqab*. It is a root word meaning to puncture or perforate, more or less with violence. As a result, some of the meanings of the word can be to appoint someone or something, sort of like 'X' marks the spot. It can mean to blaspheme, bore, curse, release expression with (holes), name, (pierce) or striking through. Even the words libel or slander can be seen in this word. It does not always have a negative meaning. Also notice that it is just the opening through which the wind or breath or water or whatever substance flows through. Before it branches off to the word *neqeb*, the word *neqe* can correspond to it, but not necessarily be rooted to it. *Neqe* means to be pure or clean. This word can branch off in many directions.

Now, jump a whole stream over and we have the word *nesa;* meaning to carry away, like an insurrection. This word is directly related to the word *nacah* (pronounced *nawsaw*), and it is where we get the Hebrew word for *burden*. That Hebrew word is *massa*. Every time you read that one of the prophets had a burden of the Lord, you are looking at part of this stream of word etymology.

The Ability of the Hebrew Language

I believe there is a point to the Lord using the words He chooses. The word *massa* gives us a burden to lift up, and we pour out the words through our mouths which are pipes that breath flows from. The enemy tries to puncture, slander or wound us so that what flows out is marred, misshapen or dual-spoken by a double-mindedness.

This is why I refuse to receive a negative word about someone unless the Lord has spoken to me first, and in many cases before I ever have trouble with a person. If you're like me, you know the pain of being set up by the devil and human beings and the trauma of the imprisonment of false accusations and slander by those who look perfect. Since we know this pain, why would we want to do the same to others? Jesus took this pain willingly, knowing that the devil is the accuser of the brethren. He became burdened for His bride long before we knew we could have that kind of relationship with God.

Isaiah 49, written over 700 years before Christ was born, says this to His people:

"But Zion said, 'The Lord hath forsaken me, and my Lord hath forgotten me.' Can a woman forget her sucking child, that she should not have compassion on the son of her womb? Yea, they may forget, yet will I not forget thee. Behold, I have graven thee upon the palms of My hands; thy walls are continually before Me. Thy children shall make haste; thy destroyers and they that made thee waste shall go forth of thee. Lift up thine eyes round about, and behold: all these gather themselves together, and come to thee. 'As I live,' saith the Lord, 'thou shalt surely clothe thee with them all, as with an ornament, and bind them on thee, as a bride doeth' " (Isaiah 49:14-18).

It is amazing to me that Jesus was punctured by nails and sword and beaten with Roman whips so that by His stripes we are healed. By His puncturing the burden of our sin-drenched souls can be made whole so that we can become His bride. As this time period of revival moves along, truths concerning the love of Christ and His bride will be heightened.

Many people have been wounded by the church. In this world, unfortunately, hurt people hurt family, and hurt life in general for other people. I believe these end-time revivals will bring about a realization that the breath of God can move through the holes in many hearts caused by that wounding and create healing out of pain. These revivals will see many speak our Lord's word from pipes that have been used to wound, and instead speak wholeness.

This can produce healing on many levels where chaos from below the ground, and its effects above ground, can experience a miraculous restoration. This newness revives our spirits and births new life. Just at the moment that we feel God has forsaken us, the holes in the palms of His hands take over. The river of life flows into us, creating something new for us by opening a path in the heavenly arena. It may start out small, but as many receive healing, it can become a flood-tide of Godly wholeness across the planet.

The Wealth of the Hebrew: Peh and Massa

Before we look at some of the last restorations from Genesis, I want to mention two Hebrew words. This understanding of breath or God's breath blowing through the pipes and light being created, is an understanding from the Hebrew word *peh*. It is commonly translated as *word* in the Old Testament. It means to blow through the mouth in speech, and by inference to scatter. It is the only Old Testament word that gives us the understanding of being two-edged. In fact, it is always fascinating for me to read Hebrew language scholars and discover how often the Lord uses one word that has several diverse meanings, almost in a two-edged way. Such is also the case with the next word we will look at.

Though not translated as 'word,' it is used so often with the phrase, 'word of the Lord' that it should be studied with commonly used phrases translated into English as 'word.' The Hebrew word is *massa*. We just looked at it. It means a burden or lifting up, and is used for the priests in lifting up their burden as an offering or as a tribute. It is especially used as a song in singing a tribute or burden lifted up as praise to the Lord.

In some Bibles it is translated as the word *oracle*. This is the word that is most commonly used in Isaiah or Jeremiah when the prophet speaks of the burden of the Lord concerning Moab or Damascus or Egypt (Isaiah 15:1; 17:1; 19:1; 21:1, 11, 13; 22:1). In Jeremiah, God chides them for asking what the burden or oracle of the Lord is (Jeremiah 23:33). The understanding here is that God is asking, "Will you really be burdened by what burdens me?" When the word *massa* is used, the understanding is always that it is the burden of the word of the Lord (Zechariah 9:1 and 12:1). Especially in the books of the prophets, we begin to understand this two-edged word concept.

Moab, Damascus and Egypt were burdens on the people or questions that the people had, and yet, it should have been a time where the people offered prayers up to the Lord in order to cast their burdens on Him. It's as if the prophets are exhorting them to do that because when that is done, it now becomes the Lord's burden.

Casting Out: Ek-ballo

The word *massa* is such a fascinating word because it is used for praise, prayer and prophesying the word of the Lord, but cannot technically be translated as 'word' because it really means 'burden.' It was Jesus' ministry that shifted the burden of the priesthood in offering sacrifices, and instead offered Himself as the sacrifice so we could be made free from the burden of demonic entanglements of sickness and oppression. It was Jesus' ministry that shifted the priesthood to speak or breathe out the words, 'In Jesus' Name, satan, I cast you out.' This phrase, *cast out*, in English is from two Greek words *ek* and *ballo*.

About 25 years ago the Lord had me in a study of demonic interference and cleaning a property of them where we had moved. I made a mistake of binding a devil on the property. The next day I came into the barn to find that thing bound by invisible, but quite real cords, and hobbling around the aisle way. I complained to the Lord about it still being there even though I had cast it out the day before. He said plainly to me that I had not cast it out, that I had bound it. So I cast it out and as soon as my chores were done, I went into the house and conducted a word study.

What I found was quite interesting. When Jesus healed the sick and cast out demons the word most often used in the Greek is this word *ek-ballo*. The first Greek word means 'out from, up, over and above' and the other means to 'cast or throw'. The understanding we get is that when you cast a demon out, it is sent into a place so far above and out of reach as to never be able to come back again. This is why demons hate being cast out.

Headwaters And The Bride

The revivals in Argentina have been known for casting out devils. I believe any end-time revival will have the word of God moving around us to such an extent that the revelation of His love for His bride, coupled with a real understanding of how to remove all demonic interlopers off His people, will be evident in our midst. These demons burden the people. They even attempt to make Christians have enough doubts to keep us as 'dual-minded' (Galatians 5:17; Romans 16:17; 1 Timothy 3:8; James 1:8, 4:8). Any end-time revival will see the effects which remove these burdens through the word of the Lord, as that word is released from the mouths of the saints.

The devil has always played for keeps, but we need to learn why God uses a dual understanding when He speaks. One word from God is so multifaceted with light-giving life, that even as we breathe Him in, we release deliverance. Hallelujah! This sets multitudes of individuals free at the same time; catching by surprise and casting out all enemy forces in the process.

Suddenly

1 Thessalonians 4:16-18: "*For the Lord himself shall descend from heaven with a shout, with the voice of the archangel, and with the trump of God: and the dead in Christ shall rise first: Then we which are alive and remain shall be caught up together with them in the clouds, to meet the Lord in the air: and so shall we ever be with the Lord. Wherefore comfort one another with these words.*"

1 Thessalonians 5:2-3: "*For yourselves know perfectly that the day of the Lord so cometh as a thief in the night. For when they shall say, Peace and safety; then sudden destruction cometh upon them, as travail upon a woman with child; and they shall not escape.*"

1 Thessalonians 5:6: "*Therefore let us not sleep, as do others; but let us watch and be sober.*"

1 Thessalonians 5:9: "*For God hath not appointed us to wrath, but to obtain salvation by our Lord Jesus Christ . . .*"

1 Thessalonians 5:12-13: "*And we beseech you, brethren, to know them which labour among you, and are over you in the Lord, and admonish you; And to esteem them very highly in love for their work's sake. And be at peace among yourselves.*"

1 Thessalonians 5:23: "*And the very God of peace sanctify you wholly; and I pray God your whole spirit and soul and body be preserved blameless unto the coming of our Lord Jesus Christ.*"

Chapter Eighteen

First Things First And Then
A Wedding Feast

The Lord gave me the title for this book suddenly! I had no idea I would be writing it. I was in the process of turning one of our popular church Bible-study guides into a book. I had been working on it for a while, thinking it would take no more than a year to finish. That's when my life went sideways suddenly about a year into it. When things finally calmed down, I only had two chapters left to write, until one Sunday church service. We were singing a song with the word *Suddenly* in it and the Lord overpowered me. Suddenly I couldn't talk, only sob and laugh and sob and laugh some more. The next day, Monday, was when the Lord revealed this book. It took a very short period of time, only about three weeks to write. That's because most of it was research and revelation the Lord had been giving me for well over twenty years. Of course, life went sideways again due to my husband's surgery. Publishing this work took many more months. Thankfully, Jesus is in charge of our lives.

Without research that came to light from recent archeological excavations, I wouldn't have been able to finish this book. The reality is that no one knows the day or the hour when our Lord will return. Unless the Holy Spirit shows us, we can't even be certain what will happen tomorrow. No one can say with certainty what revivals of any length will look like exactly until Jesus shows us. I think that's because God does not tell the devil what things will look like. He may whisper to some of us. But for me personally, it's like pillow talk. It's just too weird for people to talk about what is said between a husband and wife in the intimacy of their home.

That is what it's like for me when Jesus speaks or I have an experience with the Ancient of Days. I really can't talk about it unless Father says to share it. That's why I've shared very little about personal experiences that I have had with the Holy Spirit in this book. Unless it's necessary for a book or some other benefit for the body of Christ, and at the direction of the Spirit, there is no need to talk about the experiences of God.

The reality, though, is that these experiences are sprung on all of us *Suddenly!* What I can say with certainty is that when God makes promises in the Bible, they will come to pass. We shouldn't look for signs and wonders. Instead, we should preach the word so souls are saved and saints are discipled. The great news is that signs and wonders are a byproduct of preaching the Gospel message. The devil hates signs and wonders because he knows saints are spreading the truth and he's losing ground.

Restoring What Was Lost

In Genesis we see with each toledot heading that there is a change that takes place from what God originally created. I want to share with you some research I made that surprised me. I've mentioned the Lord has been talking to me about an end-time ingathering, practically since I was first saved. I didn't realize what He was showing me back then, but sometime around the 1990s I began to catch on. I knew He was showing me something important, but I simply didn't understand all of it.

In 2015, I was researching what I felt Jesus wanted me to say to a small church outside of dairyland in Wisconsin. I was stunned at what He was going to do with the whole region. He kept highlighting these escarpments to me in the geology of the earth. And that's when

First Things First And Then A Wedding Feast

I discovered every major revival within the last 100 years took place near a major escarpment area.[58]

Some might say that there are escarpments all over the globe, so finding them within close distances of major revivals isn't hard to do. Naturally speaking, I would agree. Nevertheless, I believe when we see toledot placements and the escarpments, we see the potential for God to reprove a spiritual condition for the earth that took place at the same time the people connected to that portion of the earth were affected. It's obvious that nothing on the earth will be free until God makes a new heaven and earth. But revivals and spiritual harvests do something in the atmosphere as well as change people in the geographic locations. The change does not usually last for long, unfortunately. That's why a new heaven and earth will be necessary.

I would like to mention that I am not trying to create some new theological discovery here. There is nothing new under the sun. Father God has been speaking to His people about restoration for centuries, even millennia. These are just observations I feel the Holy Spirit has led me to make so we may believe for God to restore some of the things that were lost on the earth. Unless we become enamored with what Jesus wants to do in this last days revival and go and do what it is He is telling us to do, I'm not sure we will see everything we have been promised. Oh, some will; but I feel the need to encourage all of us to believe for God's promises to us personally, and to the body of Christ corporately in these end times.

Former Water and New Wine

The church I was preaching at had a major escarpment within a few miles of the town it was located in. After I preached that Sunday, Mrs. Pastor (they were a husband and wife team), took me for a drive to a national park where there were plaques displaying the escarpment formations around the bodies of water. The plant life and birds were phenomenal. Being early spring in the region, everything was

---

[58] Please see the end of this book, the "For Future Reading" section.

Suddenly

coming to life. This was no small escarpment area. It was part and parcel of a range of escarpments that go from New York and the Finger Lakes through to Wisconsin, Michigan and the lakes which border it, as well as Illinois. What some term as the Third Great Awakening took place from New York to Ontario, Canada, within this same escarpment area.

Argentina has had one of the longest running revivals in history, and is located on a major escarpment region which, much like Niagara Falls, has created a large waterfall area. Every country from England and Wales through to Africa has seen revivals in some form or another near their respective escarpment. We can't skip over the revival that took place in California at the turn of the last century. The San Andreas fault flows right below it and escarpments dot the region.

One revival I thought had missed the pattern was in Pensacola, Florida. At least I thought that until research uncovered a major escarpment located in the Gulf of Mexico that stretches the whole western side of the state of Florida, and borders the Gulf from the Keys, ending just below Pensacola out into the Gulf. Two areas that haven't seen the kind of revivals we are familiar with is the Kurdish Escarpment area. They are the headwaters of the Euphrates and Tigris. The second would be the grandaddy of all rifts, escarpments and valleys, and that is the Jordan Valley.

Most scholars believe the origination of the Garden of Eden is somewhere near this Great Rift. If you look at the Jordan Valley from space you will see a deep gash or fault line in the earth. We know this tectonic activity is still ongoing just because of the deposits that are left on the landscape. It is because rain and runoff scoop up these deposits that make the Jordan a muddy river.

Ezekiel 28:13: "Thou hast been in Eden the garden of God; every precious stone was thy covering, the sardius, topaz, and the diamond, the beryl, the onyx, and the jasper, the sapphire, the emerald, and the carbuncle, and gold: the workmanship of thy tabrets and of thy pipes was prepared in thee in the day that thou wast created." We see some of the most beautiful stones on this earth as Lucifer's covering or adornments. We have no idea exactly where God got these from; the "Mountain of God" or somewhere else (Ezekiel 28:13-14). Wherever they came from, they are reflected among the geology of the earth. It is possible some are reflected in the high priest's *hoshen* (breastplate) where Urim and Thummim resided over his ephod. These represented light/judgment, authority and the twelve tribes of Israel.

Obviously all this symbolism reflects human/spiritual authority. It became defiled because of the Fall, and thus a source of contention connected below the ground. Did it correspond in some fashion by what covered Lucifer? There are ten stones mentioned and two separate instruments that work in conjunction with the stones; one producing sound and the other producing a brilliant light as breath was dispersed. That would make twelve. We see these toledoth headlining eleven places of change or contention among mankind and the earth. If you agree with me that God is the first one, and no regular toledot concerns Him because there is no contention in Him, then it is interesting that Lucifer's coverings and function have a similar number demarcation.

If they are points of contention etched in the permanent surface of the earth, I feel like the Lord uses the revivals located near them to basically tell the devil, 'your time is up and I'm restoring what's been lost.' The devil knows it becomes like it was in the beginning with water and soil. As the water cuts through soil, it takes the minerals downstream, bringing healing miles away. So it is as the Holy Spirit moves upon human flesh, healing disperses geographically. As mankind travels, this healing and anointing of the Holy Spirit spreads. Satan's game is up and he cannot contain revival waters.

Revival to the People Connected to Each Toledot

I would like to view the relatives that have had strife infuse their generations since sin entered the world. These will need revival to restore their own relationships as well as revival to restore their relationships to the rest of the world; and, to some extent, the land they occupy. Who are they now? Well, we know Ishmael's descendants to be Arabs, in general, along with Esau. Esau's family line was divided by various wives from different backgrounds; one Canaanite and one Ishmaelite (Genesis 26:34; 36:2). I believe if they connect on land and a toledot is part of their headline story, they will need some type of restoration, thus the need for revival to them.

Let me also make mention of the fact that Abraham has no toledot listed for him. Many make a big deal of this since he is the father of two groups of people. His father, sons and grandsons are mentioned. If I am correct and toledot are slightly more than just headlines; that they let us know a change took place to the extent that some kind of restoration is necessary, then not mentioning Abraham makes sense. He and Sarah both had name changes. So we know that somewhere along the line they experienced some kind of restoration by the Almighty so as not to have caused defilement in their own land.

We also know it from Jesus' words in John's Gospel: "They answered and said unto him, Abraham is our father. Jesus saith unto them, If ye were Abraham's children, ye would do the works of Abraham. But now ye seek to kill me, a man that hath told you the truth, which I have heard of God: this did not Abraham" (John 8:39-40). "Your father Abraham rejoiced to see my day: and he saw it, and was glad" (John 8:56). We know from this dialog that Abraham experienced something from God, and that whatever revelation he received concerning Jesus, ameliorated any defilement on the land. It is also obvious from this passage that his sons, or offspring certainly have had much contention among themselves within their border lands causing defilement.

Sovereignty and Marriage

I believe God is working backwards in revival to restore. By doing so He undergirds our success. Remember that the book of Revelation tells us that we overcome by the blood and the word of our testimony (Revelation 12:11). We have not seen major revivals to the original places of the earth where Adam and Eve were separated from a marriage made in heaven. I believe because of the length of time of this last-days' ingathering— I felt the Lord say 30 to 40 years— we will see many things restored that were lost or changed. This is evidenced by the headlines or *toledot* in Genesis. It would not surprise me if escarpments were found in close proximity to these revivals.

Two institutions associated with Adam and Eve that were adversely affected by the Fall were sovereignty and marriage. While Adam's sovereignty was changed, Eve was changed as well. We have yet to see a major revival affecting women to a large extent. History shows us that women were a major part of the revivals in the last one hundred years. Nevertheless, theology and full partnership has yet to materialize. The revival that occurred in Pensacola, Florida, in 1995, happened on Fathers' Day. Some have called it a revival after the Scripture seen in Malachi 4:6: "And he shall turn the heart of the fathers to the children, and the heart of the children to their fathers, lest I come and smite the earth with a curse." We have never seen something similar or noteworthy restoring a sense of motherhood.

Jesus said: "O, Jerusalem, Jerusalem, thou that killest the prophets, and stonest them which are sent unto thee, how often would I have gathered thy children together, even as a hen gathereth her chickens under her wings, and ye would not! Behold, your house is left unto you desolate. For I say unto you, Ye shall not see me henceforth, till ye shall say, Blessed is he that cometh in the name of the Lord" (Matthew 23:37-39; see also Luke 13:34-35).

I am not saying God is a woman, or a man, for that matter. He chooses to be identified by male pronouns. I am saying that there is a place within the God Head that we see characteristics of nurturing and comfort, of reproduction and sustenance that we as humans identify more with the females of the species as opposed to men (Genesis 17:1). We see this as well within the animal kingdom, as Jesus did when He mentioned gathering His brethren as a hen would her chicks. We all know the church is mentioned as the Lamb's bride and Israel is mentioned as God's wife (Exodus 19:5-8; Jeremiah 3:14;

Isaiah 54:5). We have never really had a resurgence in understanding this aspect of the character of God that is reflected in His people.

Another institution connected to the first is marriage. We have seen a proliferation in marriage conferences and teachings attempting to heal rifts within the marriage covenant. But any real infusion of the Holy Spirit within the institution which would sovereignly restore the covenant, with signs and wonders following, has yet to occur. Now, it may be that the Lord finds women as pastors with their husbands or as pastors if they are single, and the marriage conferences that have been going on as restoration enough; I don't know that. He has said nothing like that to me. I get a real sense that we will see something more for those two institutions, along with mass salvations among our Jewish brethren as a long-term revival progresses.

Let me make a supposition that you can agree or disagree with. We are now living through the blood in overcoming, faith-filled testimony on an individual basis. As we are connecting with revival or restoration to those areas of contention seen in Genesis; then defilement of land, the symbolic representation of water, motherhood, the institution of marriage, as well as deliverance among Jewish brethren, will all need a revival of sorts before the bride of Christ is "caught up" in the air for the marriage supper of the Lamb.

Sin has worked from Godly order to chaos. God is bringing His order out of what certainly is a planet caught in chaos. If nothing else, the escarpments show us how bad that chaos is. We do know that the outpouring of the Holy Spirit has always been typified as new wine and water. Revivals with the outpouring of God in glory among the descendants of Noah, Shem, Terah, Isaac, Ishmael, Esau and Jacob will bring about much peace for the land masses they live in. Much of the land that these people groups reside in is lacking in abundant water. Finding water or being able to make water in these geographic areas will bring great economic health to them.

Many years ago the Holy Spirit had me researching waterways as a whole and specifically in my own nation. I discovered, much to my dismay, how captive they had become to demonic forces. Even stories my husband shared with me concerning various nations' naval forces and how sordid life on the ships had become, reveals this bondage.

The infilling of the Holy Spirit, along with the restoration of how women should be viewed and treated in those geographic areas and within maritime-related institutions, will bring wholeness to men, women and their marriages worldwide. Any revival within those people groups which expresses wholeness to marriages and women must express Father God, fatherhood and motherhood in health and healing. It is cause and effect and has the potential to change whole land masses and waterways.

Obviously, no revival can give us a new heaven and earth. I'm not even suggesting that. We've also lost two major rivers that flowed out of the headwaters from the Garden of Eden. The body of Christ in those areas of the world have been persecuted in such a way that their health or wholeness has dried up. As just mentioned, those regions of the world are very dry, naturally. It would be a small miracle to find large underground water sources. This would bring much deliverance to the area. Unfortunately, it won't make a difference if they are still in captivity to the demonic forces which hold them hostage.

I am told that a great revival is going on among many in the Middle East, but it is being done quietly and in secret.[59] I'm looking forward to the day when the dryness we see among the Western church is infused with Holy Ghost fire, and the hidden affection of the Eastern church can merge to create a river of overflowing streams for the planet to be watered in Holy Spirit wholeness. I believe when the Holy Spirit enables the crossing of those waters, Father God may very well tell His Son that His bride is ready.

---

[59] < https://defiantamerica.com/visions-of-jesus-isis-sickened-muslims-iraq-now-they-christ/ >< https://www.charismamag.com/spirit/evangelism-missions/14442-when-muslims-see-jesus > For other archaeological digs in Nazareth < https://soundcloud.com/the-times-of-israel/toi-21-7-20 >

Suddenly

John 4:34-36: "Jesus saith unto them, My meat is to do the will of him that sent me, and to finish his work. Say not ye, There are yet four months, and then cometh harvest? Behold, I say unto you, Lift up your eyes, and look on the fields; for they are white already to harvest. And he that reapeth receiveth wages, and gathereth fruit unto life eternal: that both he that soweth and he that reapeth may rejoice together."

Chapter Nineteen

Ephesus

I've drawn patterns from Genesis and we have one last pattern to look at. Before I draw our attention to the last one, I want to look at the church in Ephesus. She was a first-things-first type for the early church and she is one for us today. I mentioned before that I have always pondered which came first, the chicken or the egg when it came to the purity of the water and the tree of life in the Garden of Eden. Was it the water that gave purity to the tree or was it the tree that lent life to the water?

Since my Christian youth, I've always enjoyed reading about the river that flowed from the throne which sent health to the nations. This is where I answered my chicken-and-egg question. The answer is it all starts with God and flows from His throne. Since God tells us the end from the beginning, is Genesis the only place we see a literal, earthly pattern and a connection to end-time revivals?

I feel Ephesus is that New Testament pattern. It is the first place Paul gives us an understanding of the spiritual headwater leadership of five-fold ministry. Correct biblical exegesis says whatever book you find a first principle in, it will flow as an understanding to the rest of what is seen concerning it. In his letter to the Ephesians, Paul lays down the foundation for what and how five-fold ministry should function, as well as the goals for the body of Christ that they should accomplish. It is also in this letter that Paul discusses some attributes of spiritual warfare.

Suddenly

The real city of Ephesus that Paul was writing to during our New Testament time period, was almost co-equaled with the capitol of Asia for a number of reasons. It was a gateway that opened Asia up to the rest of the world. It was also considered the head or birthplace of emperor worship. Paul taught about five-fold ministry from Ephesus and it is our pattern for headwater flow from Christ's throne in the New Testament.

The geographic city of Ephesus was located at the mouth of the Aegean Sea on a river that served as a caravan route from Palestine and Syria. Ephesus was the worldwide center for the cult worship of the goddess Diana, or Artemis as was its Roman/Greek names. This is what they were warring against as Christians in an effort to rid the world of demonic influence so God in glory could rest and infiltrate. This was their warfare so the Gospel could have wider and easier access to other areas on the globe.

We talked about Paul using the example of principalities as demonic rulers. Ephesus was fighting these, and how she managed in her warfare should give us some examples today for end-time harvest revivals. It should help us in understanding how to remove these rulers, while helping the bride of Christ avoid the traps laid out by these beings. The Ephesian church was hardworking, achieving and steadfast. So satan reserves one of the most sneakiest of traps for Christians of this caliber. The churches in Revelation give us examples of the traps laid out by the enemy for churches during the last days. Let's look further at the physical city of Ephesus.

The Layout

Ephesus was located on the sea with a river. If you look at a modern map today, you would not see that. Today it looks as if it is landlocked. This is why scholars call it the city of change because the sea and land were constantly changing Ephesus' dynamics. Ephesus was also a 'first' city. What I mean by that is that her location placed her as the first port of entry for Asia, and Roman governmental officials.

Ephesus

This gave it the label as the birthplace of emperor worship. As the sea rescinded, silting the river valley, Ephesus became more of a landlocked place. As she was losing her harbor, the Emperor Caracalla made an edict proclaiming Ephesus as the first port of entry for Roman ships. This custom or legend, as it became, was inscribed on a coin during Phillip's reign in AD 244-248.

Eventually Smyrna became the port city because of the loss of Ephesus' harbor. But the custom of declaring Ephesus the first landing was continued. All the religious activity, which eventually included Christian activity, centered on one hill located in Ephesus. This was called the Holy Hill. As Artemis was a huntress, the bow was a prominent part of her entourage. Because of its harbor, Ephesus curved like a bow with two points; Pion on the East and the Hill of Astyages on the West. This obvious geographic symbol was literally washed away by the hand of the One True God, Yahveh.

We have not talked about the obvious, which was the wealth of this city. Being a first port and the center for Persian, Greek and eventually Roman financial blessings as well as religious activity, Ephesus acquired much wealth throughout her changing geographic dynamics. This made any religion centered in Ephesus also quite wealthy.

We know that they must have accomplished something in the spirit realm because they had a flourishing church. That was not an easy accomplishment in a place that was the Asian stronghold of the goddess-queen-mother cult, as well as Roman-emperor worship. The spiritual warfare must have been intense, and they paid for it with their lives. It has been recorded that all martyrs coming from that portion of the world would go through Ephesus, straight to Rome to be used in the gladiator games. It would make sense that many other Christians would also pass through that route.

In a letter written by Ignatius, the bishop of Syria, during the beginning of the second century: "I ought to be trained for the contest by you in faith, in admonition, in endurance, in long suffering...." This was written about five to fifteen or so years after John wrote. Most scholars agree that Ignatius had not read John's work. He is talking about receiving emissaries from Ephesus, because he knows he will be heading to Rome for torture in the games (martyrdom). It's obvious that from the outside looking in, the Ephesian church was well received and had worldwide status among Christian circles.

Ephesus and The Revelation

John's word to the Ephesian Church: "Unto the angel of the church of Ephesus write; These things saith he that holds the seven stars in his right hand, who walketh in the midst of the seven golden candlesticks; I know thy works, and thy labour, and thy patience, and how thou canst not bear them which are evil: and thou hast tried them which say they are apostles, and are not, and hast found them liars: And hast borne, and hast patience, and for my name's sake hast labored, and hast not fainted. Nevertheless I have somewhat against thee, because thou hast left thy first love. Remember therefore from whence thou art fallen, and repent, and do the first works; or else I will come unto thee quickly, and will remove thy candlestick out of his place, except thou repent. But this thou hast, that thou hatest the deeds of the Nicolaitanes, which I also hate. He that hath an ear, let him hear what the Spirit saith unto the churches; To him that overcometh will I give to eat of the tree of life, which is in the midst of the paradise of God" (Revelation 2:1-7).

Revelation 22:1-2: "The angel showed me the river of the water of life — water as clear as crystal— pouring out from the throne of God and of the Lamb, flowing down the middle of the city's main street. On each side of the river is the tree of life producing twelve kinds of fruit, yielding its fruit every month of the year. Its leaves are for the healing of the nations" (NET Bible).

We know the Ephesians read The Revelation; part of it was addressed to them. We see that it is down the middle of the great street of the city as the river flows, that the tree of life stood on each side. The similarity could not have been lost on the Ephesians. Noted scholar, Sir William Ramsey, records in his work that Austrian exca-

Ephesus

vators in Ephesus found a "great street" that ran from the harbor to the base of the Pion. At that time it had both sea and river. It passed a great theatre and had magnificent buildings on each side.

In the Bezan text of Acts 19:28, it mentions a street in Ephesus that the rioting guild-smiths ran to, complaining about Paul and his companions. It was from this street that they easily found a large place— the theatre the Austrians excavated— to gather and argue about Paul's philosophy. This street was the mega-main street, the entrance-way-to-everything street of its day. They would have understood the nature of the tree of life on each side of the river with the great street in the middle as John mentions later on in the book. This must have excited them that something similar was in heaven.

By most historical accounts the Ephesian Christians did not move from their city until early in the fourth century, or late in the third. This is some 300 years after John received The Revelation. We also know that the aged apostle lived among them for a while. Today, if a prophet warned a church in the height of their accomplishments like John did, that individual might be considered false.

Why all this warfare and battle language? Why all this focus on the church at Ephesus? Was this written to remove one entrenched satanic ruler in geographic Ephesus alone? Or was it written as an example for all generations of Christians so they can be prepared for warfare on Christ's terms and not at the devil's behest?

I believe John told the Ephesian church of one trap among many that will be used by our enemy for the church in any age, but especially those watching and waiting and moving with the Lamb toward an end-time revival ingathering. He commended them for their works, yet he had one word from our Lord that must have sent chills down their spines. He told them that they had left their first love. I can't imagine the pain at hearing that. It had to cut them to the core. How could it have happened? The elders must have gone over their actions and begun a time of fasting and prayer, if they weren't in one already. We can be thankful our Lord shared this with John.

Suddenly

Our First Love

Revelation 2:4-5a: "Nevertheless I have somewhat against thee, because thou hast left thy first love." In the English, we read this as if they have lost their first or pure love for Christ. But the word is not the Greek word for *lost*. It is translated correctly as *left* or *departed*, even *forsaken* as some versions render it. Its dual meaning was used in the Greek language to mean a man divorcing his wife.

I realized something about this portion of Scripture that makes it like so many things about John's writings. Scholars call them *Johannine*. When they use that word they note how polyvalent his writings are. That's because in the Hebrew and similarly with John's writings, one word could be used that had several different meanings at different levels. I believe that's what we are seeing here in Revelation 2:4.

Some disagree that John the Apostle was the one who wrote the gospel bearing his name. In my opinion, he did. Some have the same problem with The Revelation. Due to the poor quality Greek, many feel that John used a scribe with little education to write while on Patmos. This postulation is due to injuries he sustained from attempted martyrdom causing an inability to keep pen in hand. If he did not write the third epistle bearing his name, someone who knew him or was told what he said wrote it years later. Either way, we don't need these to be the same author. I just happen to feel that they are. That is due to the Johannine style of his writing.

As I dug into the Greek words and the other places where I found them, I was struck with the fact that the word *agape*, Godly love, was used here. Secondly, the word *first* (*protos*) has a dual notation connected to it. In John 1:1, we read: "In the beginning was the Word, and the *Word was with God*." The Greek words, *pros ton Theon*, is translated as you see it. The words have a movement *toward* involved. Somewhat as understanding a close dance but being totally one with. It's like the understanding for the Hebrew word *davar*. It is always translated as *word*, but you get the meaning that it is a driving force that creates something out of nothing.

Ephesus

Well, here in the prologue you get a slight feel of two people who are married, dancing; they are one, but just different. When John says that they left (*hiemi*) their first (*protos*) love (*agape*), the verb is not "to lose," but *left* as in a husband leaving his wife. That is how scholars note the definition of the word *hiemi*. Next, the same word seen in John's prologue (*pros*) is from the word we see here, *pro*. It means to be before something, first in time and space and rank. The word in the prologue is from this word, just a lot more intense. What we see in the warning to the Ephesian church is that they left their love for God, but the dual understanding is that they left God's love for them. This makes total sense that it is not a one-way-only thought.

In Thessalonians Paul, Sylvanus and Timothy address the church. The three of them had done much in Asia to raise up the work of God. They write this to them: "Remembering without ceasing your *work of faith*, and *labour of love*, and *patience of hope* in our Lord Jesus Christ, in the sight of God and our Father; Knowing, brethren *beloved*, your election of God" (1 Thessalonians 1:3-4).

The exact same Greek words are used for the Ephesian church in Revelation: work, labor and patience. John relates our Lord's words: "I know thy works, and thy labour, and thy patience." Only Paul adds a descriptive element in Thessalonians. It is not just work, labor and patience but faith, love and hope. Does that sound familiar? That's because Paul uses similar language in 1 Corinthians 13, the famous *love* chapter. Also, we see that Paul says to the Thessalonians that they are beloved. John's name means graced of God. Many have interpreted this as beloved and call John the beloved disciple.

If I am correct and the Ephesians forgot Christ's love for them, it moved them to works, labor and patience. Those are not bad things; but it shifted them to forget how much the Savior loved them. This in turn got them more focused on work, labor and patience. It moved them ever so slightly from love, hope and thus faith. Before they knew it, they had left their first love. They removed God's reality of His love for them. I can't stress enough how much God loves us. This must be our reality day and night!

As always, we have a backward view of things. If I forget how much Jesus loves me, I work my butt off to get closer, when in fact, He is closer than a breath. I then work when I need to rest in Him and who He is. This 'works effort' moves me farther away from my first love and closer to forgetting faith involved in how much He loves me. I then labor and eventually labor for a hope I already possess.

Wolves in the Last Days' Church

As I was delving into this portion of Scripture, I shared it with the brethren, and one of them mentioned that the Spirit had shown her a word about wolves among the flock in the last days' churches. She was blown away with what the Lord had shown me that morning. I was blown away with what the Lord showed us as we spoke concerning wolves. As is our habit, we hit the Scriptures together.

We're told that there will be a great falling away in the church during the end times (2 Thessalonians 2:3). I believe it is connected to what John said to the Ephesian church. We know it was important because it bothered Paul so much that he visited them before heading to Jerusalem, reminding them of how much he had talked about it. In Acts 20:16-38, we have a dialog between Paul and the elders from Ephesus.

As he would be leaving them, he mentions how he reminded them of what would happen when he was gone: "For I know this, that after my departing shall grievous wolves enter in among you, not sparing the flock. Also of your own selves shall men arise, speaking perverse things, to draw away disciples after them. Therefore watch, and remember, that by the space of three years I ceased not to warn every one night and day with tears" (Acts 20:29-31).

For three years, day and night he warned them! If it was just Ephesus and Ephesus alone, I'm not sure that the Holy Spirit would have moved Paul in such a way. I believe the early apostles were seeing something that is a real problem for the body of Christ today. First, he reminds them of his example. He talks about the fact that he took

Ephesus

directly from the counsel of God and gave the word to them personally. Then he talks about how he was burdened for their wellbeing, to the point of tears. Next, he talks about the reality that he did not covet the money, clothes or necessities of the sheep, but worked himself to provide for his needs. He tells them that this is how they must be leaders among the sheep.

To me, this is the opposite of what a wolf is. As we look at the church worldwide today, I see many who want more and more goodies. Thankfully, there are honest men and women among God's people. Unfortunately, we have some who are anything but, and they have led many away from the Lord because of it.

Paul says this to Timothy: "Now the Spirit speaks expressly, that in the latter times some shall depart from the faith, giving heed to seducing spirits, and doctrines of devils; Speaking lies in hypocrisy; having their conscience seared with a hot iron; Forbidding to marry, and commanding to abstain from meats . . ." (1 Timothy 4:1-3).

Again Paul says this: "This know also, that in the last days perilous times shall come. For men shall be lovers of their own selves, covetous, boasters, proud, blasphemers, disobedient to parents, unthankful, unholy; Without natural affection, truce breakers, false accusers, incontinent, fierce, despisers of those that are good; Traitors, heady, high-minded, lovers of pleasures more than lovers of God; Having a form of godliness, but denying the power thereof: from such turn away" (2 Timothy 3:1-5).

Peter tells us this: "Knowing this first, that there shall come in the last days scoffers, walking after their own lusts, And saying, Where is the promise of his coming? For since the fathers fell asleep, all things continue as they were from the beginning of the creation" (2 Peter 2:3-4).

It is just a slight shift from abiding in the love of Christ toward us in His faith, His hope and His love, to working our butts off for some new church program. Add to this trap the deceit other apostles warned about concerning wolves among the sheep, and we have an end-time church in real trouble.

Love Builds a Home

The Ephesian church was watching, like we are today, for that call up to our marriage feast. With the letter from John, they had the courage to go forward once they realized that a city like their own on earth would be awaiting them. They must have realized something else. As I was sitting before the Lord pondering what I was reading, I understood the garden that Adam and Eve lived in was their home. In our world today a garden is not the home.

A home always has an atmosphere. Many men don't realize this when they marry. The Bible tells men not to marry a contentious woman as it will affect their lives forever (Proverbs 21:19; 27:15-16). Women also have heartache if they marry a fool for a husband. Abagail knew that when she went to save her husband, Nabal (1 Samuel 25:2-38). She told David quite plainly: "Let not my lord, I pray thee, regard this man of Belial, even Nabal: for as his name is, so is he; Nabal is his name, and folly is with him: but I thine handmaid saw not the young men of my lord, whom thou didst send" (1 Samuel 25:25). We get the impression from the passage that she was always mopping up after him.

That's when it dawned on me. What if a marriage in wholeness maintained the habitat where Adam and Eve lived? We know the overriding presence of God made that anointing possible. Yet, something changed the whole planet when Adam and Eve's covenant was broken with God. It also disrupted their covenant with one another. We know from Genesis the resultant chaos changed the water flow and the tree of life had to be cut off to them. They were kicked out of their home.

What better way to understand the marriage supper of the Lamb and the catching away of the bride in the rapture? What better way to understand the word from John to the Ephesian church of leaving their first love? What is the result of first love if not a wedding feast?

We then see in Revelation, after the marriage supper of the Lamb, a city instead of a garden. We know no temple is in it because the Lord God and the Lamb are the Temple (Revelation 21:22). They are our new abode. The Scripture, "In Him we live and move and have our being," takes on a whole new meaning; not just for our futures, but for our NOW (Acts 17:27-28)!

We also know that a new river flows from a new home where the Bride and the Lamb are present. We know new and precious stones are within its walls. We read there are gates of pearl which are left open as entry to the city and no night is ever in the city (Revelation 21:18-25). In Chapter 18, we mentioned the gems connected to each Israeli tribe in the high priest's breastplate as a possible connection to Lucifer and the connection to our earth. Jesus came to give us spiritual authority for this earth by reason of His sacrifice. We function in an authority of grace that Adam and Eve knew nothing about. It reveals both light and revelation of Godly authority satan cannot overcome.

We're told in Revelation 2:17, that we who overcome will receive a new, white stone with a name written on it. Just as all of this reminds us what was lost, all of it shows us the new grace we function in now, and the awesome promise of what is to come. The old hymnal got it right: "There's a new name written down in glory, and it's mine; O, yes, it's mine!" The very cornerstone that Mosaic Law proponents have rejected has become our sure foundation. A strong tower to run to in every situation in the here and now, and in the ages to come.

There is one last encouragement recorded by John, and it's a new tree of life whose leaves give healing for the nations. But what precipitates all this? Is it a marriage feast?

Suddenly

John 2:1-2: "And the third day there was a marriage in Cana of Galilee; and the mother of Jesus was there: And both Jesus was called, and his disciples, to the marriage."

Chapter Twenty

The Galilean Wedding

Just like the Ephesians got a word about their earthly patterns and the patterns in heaven, I believe the tiny town of Galilee got a similar word directly from our Lord. I never would have been able to connect these dots were it not for recent ancient excavations revealed in a new movie documentary being shown to the body of Christ worldwide last year (2020) and again this year.[60]

I hope I have made it crystal clear that there is no way we can do a worldwide revival on our own. As it stands now, the enemy has been attempting to short-circuit this in-gathering revival. Seeing his patterns back in 2008, our church began to rebuke that, proclaiming that the blood of Jesus was against a one-world government and that its time was not yet. Unfortunately, that thing will have a time, but not at the expense of an end-time harvest revival. We have to be adamant in receiving nothing less than what our Lord promised us.

When we understand what Jesus promised us is part of wedding betrothal promises— as God made with Israel in Exodus 19:5-8— we would understand how important it is to stand firm in what we are to receive. This is why I've included the information this research found concerning the cultural differences in the Galilee from other Jewish enclaves during Christ's time when He walked the face of the earth.

---

[60] http://www.beforethewrath.com

Suddenly

We have such a hope and strong word of encouragement from the word of God. We must not be moved from His love. Let's see what else we can garner from this research.

The Galilean Differences

For many years most scholars assumed that a Galilean wedding was exactly the same as all Jewish weddings. But recent archeological discoveries have since blown those thoughts apart.[61] For one thing, the marriage doesn't begin with them walking down the aisle, or even with a feast. It begins at the city gates where all the important business took place. Since it was a busy place, there would be many witnesses to this marriage contract. Once the covenant was agreed upon by the fathers, the groom would pour a cup of wine for the bride. If she drank from the cup, she agreed to the terms. If not, the espousal was off. She had the ultimate choice. This differed from other Jewish weddings.

If all was agreed upon then they were betrothed. This lasted anywhere from one to two years. That's because Galilee was a small town, far from the main merchant markets. The bride would go her way and the groom his, both back to their fathers' houses. Both bride and groom had jobs to do that required purchasing quite a few items. Because of the remote distance, it could take quite some time to acquire all the products necessary to satisfy the groom's father that all was ready. That and what follows next are the other differences in the Galilean wedding.

I Go to Prepare a Place for You

The groom would go to his father's house and add rooms to it in order to make a home for them. It wasn't until the groom had built the home and purchased all necessary items for the inside of it, that he

---

[61] One of the towns excavated for the documentary is Korazim. It is a national park. To see that go here: < https://www.parks.org.il/en/reserve-park/korazim-national-park >< To see an interesting post from Korazim < https://drbarrick.org/2020/12/israel-research-trip-post-11 >

could pester his father for the okay to go get his bride. But the father was quite secretive about when that could happen. He was the only one that knew the time and the hour.

In the meantime, the bride was getting herself ready. Dresses had to be made for herself and her bridesmaids. While this was happening, the groom would send his bride gifts to keep his memory before her and to let her know how much he loved and cared for her. This was also different from other Jewish wedding customs. The next thing that was different was that while this was all going on, the Galilean bride was considered set apart and consecrated. It was known that she was bought for a price. When she went out, she would wear a veil to signify this.

Another difference would be how the groom would come for the bride. Since the groom's father was the only one who knew when the feast would take place, the bride and her bridesmaids had to be ready at all hours of the night. The phrase, *to come like a thief in the night* is how the groom coming for the bride was known. Because of this, Galilean brides would wear their dresses to sleep at night as the day got closer. The bridesmaids and other family members would have lamps trimmed since they had very little notice in the middle of the night to get ready.

We'll Meet Him in the Air

When the father told his son it was time to go get his bride, he and his mates would go through the streets blowing a ram's horn to let the community know they were coming. The groom would send one ahead to let the bride's family know they were coming, but it was a sudden communication.

The bride did not walk to the groom's house. She was put on a litter and lifted up into the air. This Galilean difference was called 'flying the bride home.' Once the hoopla was known throughout the streets that a wedding feast was afoot, everyone wanted to be a part of it. All guests would have to come out into the streets dressed appropriately or else they would be unable to attend the wedding party. This was a big deal because nobody wanted to miss the bride leaving. If they did not do this and they missed the entourage when the groom brought the bride back to the father's house, the door would be closed and no one could get in. In other words, if you were late or unprepared, it was tough luck.

For seven days they celebrated while the bride and groom were also closeted away for seven days in their rooms. At the end of seven days, the groom would introduce the bride to the community. Who knew that such a small community would have a wedding ceremony that matched our Christian doctrines of communion, the baptism of the Holy Spirit with the evidence of speaking with other tongues, the gifts of the Holy Spirit, the rapture and the marriage supper of the Lamb. All the disciples save Judas were Galileans.

Being reminded of our betrothal to our Lord, and waiting for His soon return was something our first pastor and last pastor talked about frequently. I don't hear too much about the rapture from preachers any more. To be honest, it's been since December of 2018, that I preached a message about it myself.

Watching the documentary and doing the research for this chapter has challenged me to be more mindful of the coming of our Lord. As you can see from a Galilean wedding, being shut up for seven days with the groom is a pre-tribulation theology. It's the one I was taught as a young Christian. I've never had any problems with it.

I know people argue about these things incessantly. I leave people to their own opinions. If we are truly blood-bought and Holy Spirit filled, then arguing about this is not a good use of our time here on earth, especially since the day approaches sooner rather than later. As the Galilean said, "It will come as a thief in the night!"

Suddenly

Romans 10:8-10: "But what saith it? The word is nigh thee, even in thy mouth, and in thy heart: that is, the word of faith, which we preach; That if thou shalt confess with thy mouth the Lord Jesus, and shalt believe in thine heart that God hath raised him from the dead, thou shalt be saved. For with the heart man believeth unto righteousness; and with the mouth confession is made unto salvation."

Romans 8:21-22: "Because the creature itself also shall be delivered from the bondage of corruption into the glorious liberty of the children of God. For we know that the whole creation groaneth and travaileth in pain together until now. And not only they, but ourselves also, which have the first-fruits of the Spirit, even we ourselves groan within ourselves, waiting for the adoption, to wit, the redemption of our body."

Romans 10:11: "For the scripture saith, Whosoever believeth on him shall not be ashamed."

Chapter Twenty-One

Final Thoughts

We have strayed so far from God's goals. I'm so thankful Jesus came to show us how to function by watching Father God speak to situations on earth and see creation respond, produce and even replicate healing. Jesus said he did nothing except He saw the Father do it. God still needs to teach us how to speak His word. We still must be mindful of following Jesus so we are not seduced by serpents of pride, greed and lust. This is why it's so critical for five-fold ministry to do things God's way, with God's idea; not some "good" idea of doing things.

I'm sensing this end-time harvest will reach all walks of life. The blessing of revival to nations, while spiritual and on an individual level, will also extend to finance and commerce as well as other business sectors. I'm disgusted every time the Lord opens a door of opportunity for me to talk to someone in business and all they can share is the depravity going on in offices, on job sites, in areas of higher education, as well as transportation. Many years ago a brother, who worked in the merchant marine sector, shared how awful it is to live on a vessel with nothing but debauchery and obscenity all over the whole ship. Not long thereafter the Lord began to show me the demonic activity involved on our waters.

I could spend reams sharing the infiltration of enemy forces in so many sectors of commerce, business and government. I choose instead to share God's goal of using blood-bought saints to kick these intruding interlopers off our planet and away from human endeavors that they have captured. When we do, I believe we will see new technologies propel nations forward in prosperity. Their trades, merchants, bankers and various other undertakings will be revived with God-infused ideas birthed in the heat of revival kindling.

I am relating much of what I'm sensing in a generalized way. That's because none of us can assume because God came in revival one way, it is going to be the same again. When I speak about revival, ingathering, harvest and restoration, I want to remove from our thinking what any of that will look like exactly. I've tried to describe concepts as opposed to actual and specific happenings.

Revival is nothing more than an open heaven sown by a people declaring God's word in song, praise, worship, prose, prayer or message. Share the Gospel and signs and wonders are going to follow. It's like a river; if you are connected to a headwater, you cannot help but have a river. If we don't do church God's way, we will have these great social programs, but they will not produce the Holy Spirit atmosphere of revival harvest that changes the very hearts and souls of mankind. Signs and wonders are great tools, but they won't get people saved. Sharing Jesus, the Word made flesh, will. Signs and wonders attract people. Once you've got their attention, Jesus must be preached. We must see the word, see Jesus.

Almost every major Christian denomination started from some revival; some image of God or revelation of Father, Son and Holy Spirit that had been lost and needed restoration. Yet it doesn't take us long to start worshiping what we can see; in other words, the revival or the physical manifestation of the truth. We assume that's not so bad. But as soon as we take our eyes off of the person of the Word in Jesus Christ, we backslide.

At the turn of the 1900s a revival took place that produced three new Pentecostal denominations. The work of the Holy Spirit was restored with the evidence of speaking with other tongues. These denominations have done wonderful works for Christ and are quite

Final Thoughts

faithful in what they do today. But a while back I was in a church service listening to a minister quote from research that found forty percent of those attending Spirit-filled churches never speak in other tongues. This research also found that twenty-four percent don't believe the Bible is the literal word of God.[62] The reality of those findings horrified me.

We have within Christianity today many various groups, all worshipping in one way or another with various experiences, even with signs and wonders as they worship. I just keep getting this impression that the world may begin to look very dark, but the saints will echo a cry. Each group will hear from the Spirit, asking Him to come. This very sacrifice will waft up to our High Priest, Jesus. True worship always brings Father God to alight on living sacrifices. It is the aroma of the fear of the Lord. When Father and Son "smell" this incense, it will bring them as fire on our altars (Romans 12:1-3). When Father smells this, He will tell His Son, Jesus, It Is Time!

As I've made clear, this is one reason why we cannot "mix" or cross denominational streams as we desire. As the fear of the Lord is heightened in all camps, Jesus will come and ignite the workers in the fields of the earth for harvest. Many will realize the walls that divide us are not from God. Denominations that refused the infilling will become Spirit-filled churches. The streams will cross so it becomes one long, end-time harvest revival/ingathering. As He moves among each denomination and repentance is made and more are added to the churches daily, the breaking of bread will elicit an understanding of the marriage supper of the Lamb.

That revelation will give all of us what kind of 'New Man' we are in Christ. We will have a burden to be one again: new Jewish believers, along with the multitudes of Christian denominations. All will realize the need to accept Christ's death, burial and resurrection and all will invite the Holy Spirit to live in and among us. I believe God will accept that prayer of sacrifice and alight on it. We will see one huge

---

[62] https://www.pewforum.org/2006/10/05/spirit-and-power/

Suddenly

ground swell river. Each will worship in their respective places all around the world, each having a *kairos* moment with every *parousia* of Christ. It could very well be that we may see the final catching up: the final *parousia*.

Frequently while writing this book I felt impressed that our Lord is coming to catch His bride away quickly; sooner than many think. Some might wonder why I felt timeline in-gatherings would take 30 to 40 years. When I questioned the Lord, I received confirmation as well as the reality that many will miss accepting Christ now. They will accept Christ after the bride has been caught up, thus experiencing the tribulation. This book will encourage them to seek Christ for souls. They will need signs and wonders, even with anti-Christ seeking their heads. Many will do so at the point of martyrdom.

Without a constant reality that nothing can be done without His sustaining grace, we are incapable as humans to receive this. Thankfully, we have a miracle-working God all too capable to reside within us to accomplish this and help us receive all He has spoken. All we need to do is believe, receive; obey and be available to love. The Spirit and the Bride say, 'Come, Lord Jesus!'

Epilogue

Revelation 5:5-14: "And one of the elders saith unto me, Weep not: behold, the Lion of the tribe of Juda, the Root of David, hath prevailed to open the book, and to loose the seven seals thereof. And I beheld, and, lo, in the midst of the throne and of the four beasts, and in the midst of the elders, stood a Lamb as it had been slain, having seven horns and seven eyes, which are the seven Spirits of God sent forth into all the earth. And he came and took the book out of the right hand of him that sat upon the throne. And when he had taken the book, the four beasts and four and twenty elders fell down before the Lamb, having every one of them harps, and golden vials full of odours, which are the prayers of the saints. And they sung a new song, saying, Thou art worthy to take the book, and to open the seals thereof: for thou wast slain, and hast redeemed us to God by thy blood out of every kindred, and tongue, and people, and nation; And hast made us unto our God kings and priests: and we shall reign on the earth. And I beheld, and I heard the voice of many angels round about the throne and the beasts and the elders: and the number of them was ten thousand times ten thousand, and thousands of thousands; Saying with a loud voice, Worthy is the Lamb that was slain to receive power, and riches, and wisdom, and strength, and honor, and glory, and blessing. And every creature which is in heaven, and on the earth, and under the earth, and such as are in the sea, and all that are in them, heard I saying, Blessing, and honor, and glory, and power, be unto him that sitteth upon the throne, and unto the Lamb for ever and ever. And the four beasts said, Amen. And the four and twenty elders fell down and worshipped him that liveth for ever and ever."

Suddenly

Future Reading

The websites listed are under the aegis of many different groups. The author/publisher of this book make no representation concerning the accuracy or ideology of these sites. Because of the fluidity of the Internet, the URLs may or may not be available by the time you access them.

http://www.geologyin.com/2021/03/scientists-detect-signs-of-hidden.html

For other archaeological digs in Nazareth:
https://soundcloud.com/the-times-of-israel/toi-21-7-20

Earth has 5 layers:
http://www.geologyin.com/2021/03/scientists-detect-signs-of-hidden.html

Super rare minerals only on earth:
http://www.geologyin.com/2016/02/super-rare-minerals-make-earth-unique.html

10 facts about San Andreas fault:
http://www.geologyin.com/2016/02/did-you-know-10-facts-about-san-andreas.html

Definitions from geological points and you can see the ones formed through tectonic action, water action and those in the sea bed:

https://www.sciencedirect.com/topics/earth-and-planetary-sciences/escarpment
http://worldlandforms.com/landforms/escarpment/

Future Reading

For children reading this book looking for more on escarpments from around the world:

Africa's escarpments are formed mainly from headwater erosion of rivers:

https://askinglot.com/what-process-formed-the-great-escarpment

https://askinglot.com/open-detail/41393 226

https://www.yonkerspublicschools.org/cms/lib/NY01814060/Centricity/Domain/1614/Earth%20Processes%20and%20P_P%20and%20C%20Teacher%20Copy.pdf

For some of the best geology maps out there:

https://geology.com/world/middle-east.shtml

Areas of Major Escarpments:

Kentucky:
https://www.geocaching.com/geocache/GC1GQYY_the-pottsville-escarpment

Southern Africa:
https://en.wikipedia.org/wiki/Great_Escarpment,_Southern_Africa

New York/Canada/Illinois/Wisconsin/Michigan:
https://www.britannica.com/place/Niagara-Escarpment

Southern Oregon:
https://www.southernoregon.com/lakes/lakeabert/index.html

Florida; Out in the Gulf, from Pensacola to the Keys on the western coast (Gulf of Mexico):

Suddenly

https://oceanexplorer.noaa.gov/okeanos/explorations/ex1803/logs/may1/welcome.html

South America, form along with the Iguazu Falls waterfall and other geography covering the countries of Argentina, Brazil, Peru, Chile and Uruguay:

https://www.researchgate.net/publication/281414105_The_Iguazu_falls_Brazil-Argentina

The Middle East:

https://www.worldwildlife.org/ecoregions/at1302

https://transcaucasiantrail.org/en/hike/dilijan-national-park-armenia/map-trail-notes/

https://en.m.wikipedia.org/wiki/Southwestern_Arabian_foothills_savanna

https://www.nationsonline.org/oneworld/map/saudiarabia-map.htm

The Great Rift Valley:

https://en.wikipedia.org/wiki/Great_Rift_Valley

All others:

https://web.itu.edu.tr/~okay/makalelerim/67%20-%20ergene%20meric%20-%20JGSL%202002.pdf

https://www.offshore-mag.com/home/article/16762472/middle-east-geology-why-the-middle-east-fields-may-produce-oil-forever

Book:
https://www.sciencedirect.com/book/9780444824653/sedimentary-basins-and-petroleum-geology-of-the-middle-east

Future Reading

More websites:
https://www.usgs.gov/center-news/imaging-israel-s-dead-sea-fault-understand-how-continents-stretch-and-rift

https://link.springer.com/article/10.1007/s12665-013-2373-4

https://qjegh.lyellcollection.org/content/qjegh/11/1/1.full.pdf

https://www.geoexpro.com/articles/2018/03/the-best-geological-site-in-the-middle-east

https://www.britannica.com/place/Tigris-Euphrates-river-system

https://www.academia.edu/32218665/Sedimentology_and_Stratigraphy_of_Bekhme_Formation_Upper_Cretaceous_in_Selected_Sections_in_Kurdistan_Region_Iraq

https://www.sciencedirect.com/science/article/abs/pii/S0012821X17301760

https://pubs.geoscienceworld.org/gsa/geosphere/article/16/5/1107/588245/Tectonic-geomorphology-and-Plio-Quaternary

https://www.cambridge.org/core/journals/geological-magazine/article/abs/palaeoenvironmental-analysis-of-a-miocene-basin-in-the-high-taurus-mountains-southern-turkey-and-its-palaeogeographical-and-structural-significance/F091C708DAB2449369A2C1AAEDB12342

Galilean Society:

https://www.ancient-origins.net/news-history-archaeology/golan-heights-0011673
https://www.baslibrary.org/biblical-archaeology-review/33/4/10
https://www.baslibrary.org/biblical-archaeology-review/43/4/3

https://www.baslibrary.org/biblical-archaeology-review/46/4/5

Suddenly

https://www.biblicalarchaeology.org/daily/ancient-cultures/ancient-cultures/ancient-israel/2000-year-old-mikveh-found-in-lower-galilee/
Excavations at Magdala:

https://www.worldhistory.org/aticle/1219/the-archaeological-excavations-at-magdala/

Church of the apostles found:

https://www.foxnews.com/science/church-of-the-apostles-discovered-archaeologists-say

Hezekiah's Siloam tunnel system as well as other discoveries:

https://ffoz.org/discover/israel-history/stealing-the-past.html

https://www.greatarchaelology.com/Galilee_boat.php

https://drbarrick.org/2020/12/israel-research-trip-post-11

https://www.parks.org/il/en/reserve-park/korazim-national-park

https://www.livescience.com/40046-holy-land-archaeological-finds.html

https://www.jewishvirtuallibrary.org/the-synagogue-at-capernaum

http://www.israelandyou.com/korazim/

https://www.timesofisrael.com/talmud-era-winepress-mosaic-unearthed-in-jewish-village-condemned-by-jesus/

Books:

I can't stress enough the need to read the Bible. Any future reading must include reading your Bible. There are enough translations out there for you to find one that suits your skills as well as needs. It is

Future Reading

by reading the written word of God that He can speak to you. It is through the written word of God that you understand His love for you. It is by soaking up the written words on the page of your Bible that you learn your destiny, or why you were born.

While your needs and skill level will change over the course of your life, thus the Bibles you may read will change, if you are a Christian, you will never stop reading your Bible. You will always need your Bible, no matter who or what tries to tell you differently.

Suddenly

Back Page

Thank you for reading this, my third book. I've written two others that may bless you and further your walk in Christ. To find them, you can go to the websites below. I have a fourth one available by pre-order only. It will ship by 2022 or 2023.

revchrismeier.com

'Beyond Strongholds: Infiltration By The Glory of God' examines major strongholds which prevent God in glory from abiding. Available by paperback only, it can be requested through the website or by donation to the ministry at ccm4www.org

'70 Years of American Captivity: The Polity of God, The Birth of a Nation and The Betrayal of Government' is a warning, not a prophecy. It examines the simplicity of the founding governmental documents for America and how to make sure we don't lose those civil rights. It is available by ebook, paperback and hardcover through the above websites, and on Amazon, or anywhere books are sold.

Ephesians 6:10:

"Finally, my brethren, be strong in the Lord, and in the power of his might."

Ephesians 6:13:

"Wherefore take unto you the whole armor of God, that ye may be able to withstand in the evil day, and having done all, to stand."

www.ingramcontent.com/pod-product-compliance
Lightning Source LLC
Chambersburg PA
CBHW072152100526
44589CB00015B/2201